T0334976

African Literature Today

A review
Edited by Eldred Durosimi Jones

Number 7: Focus on Criticism

JAMES CURREY

© Contributors 1975

All Rights Reserved. Except as permitted under current legislation
no part of this work may be photocopied, stored in a retrieval system,
published, performed in public, adapted, broadcast,
transmitted, recorded or reproduced in any form or by any means,
without the prior permission of the copyright owner

First published by Heinemann Educational Books 1975
Reprinted 1979

First published in the United States of America 1975
by Africana Publishing Corporation

James Currey, Woodbridge, Suffolk

ISBN 978 1 84701 120 6

Transferred to digital printing

James Currey is an imprint of Boydell & Brewer Ltd
PO Box 9, Woodbridge, Suffolk IP12 3DF, UK
and of Boydell & Brewer Inc.
668 Mt. Hope Avenue, Rochester NY 14620, USA
website: www.boydellandbrewer.com

This publication is printed on acid-free paper

Contents

Comments

Reviews

Editorial

African Literature is of primary concern to Africans and one would naturally expect to hear much on the subject from African critics. They may start with a fund of empathy with African authors coming from similar backgrounds, and they may have readier access to useful background knowledge. But even these sources of knowledge are not closed to diligent non-African scholars, who can make their own distinct contributions to the appreciation of African literature. In any case African writers have been subject to non-African influences, as – to give but one example – Okigbo's testimony in his Introduction to *Labyrinths* makes clear. Having viewed Okigbo's poetry with Anozie who had, as it were, a ringside seat, the view of Peter Thomas, who seems to have actually held the towel at crucial stages, should add to our fuller understanding of that poet who was once so 'obscure' but who now – thanks to persistent examination – is far less of a closed book even to non-poets.

That the views of African critics on African literature are not universally accepted by other Africans is easily deducible from reading *African Literature Today*. By relaxing critical vigilance African critics can stray as far from sound judgement as their non-African counterparts. *African Literature Today* hopes to provide a means by which critics of all shades can hone each other's roughnesses and provide signposts to sound critical evaluation.

As critics we must constantly remind ourselves that the central document is the work itself. It must eventually be judged by what it contains or what can legitimately be implied from it. A work of art cannot be rescued from its own deficiencies by appeals to its background. *African Literature Today* has always aimed to be a forum for discussion, and discussion implies the airing of different opinions. Not surprisingly some opinions have provoked strong reactions. Indeed where there is time reactions are deliberately sought so that differing views can appear close to each other. In this number, which focuses on general critical questions, Lindfors reacts to views expressed in *ALT* 5 by Emenyonu and Gareth Griffiths, kissing the rod of the latter, or at least fondling it, while turning it vigorously against the former. Iyasere is equally forthright in reaction to the question also latent in the conflicting views of Adeola James and Palmer.

It is easy to dismiss questions like these as naive but they continually crop up among people who actually teach African literature, and those who appoint them to do so. To that extent therefore they need to be thrashed out and *African Literature Today* is happy to serve as a threshing floor.

Emenyonu in a recent letter reminded me of two Igbo proverbs which critics would do well to keep in mind. 'The world is like a mask dancing; if you want to see it you must not stand in one place' and 'Wisdom is like a goatskin bag; every man carries his own'.

ALT 8 will focus mainly on drama. A number of articles have been specifically requested for it. Anyone who wishes to send in a spontaneous contribution is requested to write first to the editor proposing a topic before submitting it. It is proving difficult to handle unsolicited contributions which cannot be fitted into the scope of a particular number. Senders of unsolicited articles should provide postage if they wish to have their articles returned.

Contributors are requested to submit articles typewritten on quarto size paper, in double spacing and with inch-wide left and right margins. Notes should be numbered and inserted at the end; they should cite publishers in both the United Kingdom and the United States of America, as well as Africa in relevant cases.

ARTICLES

The State of
Criticism in African Literature

D. S. Izevbaye

It is now just a little over a decade since the publication of Jahn's *Muntu*
(1961), Mphahlele's *The African Image* (1962) and Gerald Moore's *Seven
African Writers* (1962).[1] Seen against the background of that early post-
independence period with its urgent drive for cultural revival these works
now take on special significance because they touch in varying degrees on
each of the following three vital issues involved in the search for an
African aesthetic: the nature of African traditional philosophy, Africa's
political image, and the European emphasis in criticism. Gerald Moore's
book was the first English criticism of African literature. It is still quoted
for its stout defence of Tutuola against the 'welter of misguided admiration
and abuse' by white and black readers alike (p. 39). Moore was a sympathetic critic. But his emphasis was often European in a way which did not
reveal the contemporary protest against European viewpoints which we
find, for example, in Achebe's 1962 article.[2] Moore could argue, for
example, that 'Tutuola seems to acknowledge no masters' (not even
Fagunwa?), and his linking of Tutuola with Bunyan and Dante rather than
with Yoruba folktales met objections then as it still does occasionally.
Ekwensi, whom he links with urban America (p. xvii), has been placed
more comfortably in the Onitsha literary milieu. A revealing example
of these two attitudes is found in the following appreciations of the way
that Africans use European languages. Gerald Moore referred to the
'new feeling for English rhythms' (p. xviii), while Jahn thought that the
rhythm and melody was African.[3]

If the tone of *Seven African Writers* carried the assurance of one
drawing his confidence from an accepted metropolitan tradition, Jahn and
Mphahlele were concerned with attitudes and prejudices that would

1

affect the future in Africa. Their two books present a literary aspect of the political atmosphere of the time. The two political attitudes to which they relate, the revaluation of the African past and the political solutions to what Mphahlele described as the 'underdog mentality' (p. 16), were offered as sources of nourishment for new literary attitudes in Africa.

The more vital of the two trends was the development of socialist ideas not merely as an ideal political philosophy which Africans would (hopefully) embrace, but primarily as a metaphor adapted from Karl Marx to describe the relationship between rich and poor nations and to offer a course of action. Its philosophy was provided in Fanon's third world manifesto, *The Wretched of the Earth*, published in 1962 like *The African Image*.

Négritude was the more controversial of the two ideas. Although a historical view of our recent past has made us see and accept the corrective function of this philosophy, it would be necessary here to try to describe what marks it has left on criticism today. Its most objectionable bequest was the acceptance, in a more positive form, of the European image of the African people as a child race to whom one might turn for a study of origins. This acceptance led to those simple polarities like innocence – corruption, simplicity – sophistication, the spontaneous – the blasé, etc. The Négritude mystique has proved too vague to be of practical value to the practice of criticism, and Jahn's most enduring works are now his *Bibliography of Neo-African Literature* and his *History of Neo-African Literature* rather than his *Muntu*.

On the positive side, however, what the Négritude movement was doing was in line with what was happening all round Africa in the '60s, although it adopted a more sensational presentation. The 1960s saw the rejection of Prospero's Africa in the light of evidence from contemporary traditional African cultures. The African historian of the time was also pointing out that there was a continuity of African traditional institutions even during colonial rule.[4]

There is a logical link here between the Négritude quest for a vital African culture and Fanon's socialist defence of the masses, who in many areas of Africa have been in this continuous stream. This argument – it largely ignored the non-literate native rulers – became the basis of the attack on the African bourgeoisie by Ngugi at Ife in 1968 and Achebe at Texas in 1969.[5] In both these attacks the Western-educated elite was presented as a renegade group. Since the criticism was made at a literary gathering in both cases, we may ignore its political implications and look at its implications for criticism, especially the growing reaction against Western attitudes in criticism,[6] as opposed to what is now a development of the Western point of view. This may appear to be a simplification.

2

But a glance at the opening paragraphs in Ravenscroft's *Chinua Achebe* will show a belief that the reference point for African writers is 'the chosen tongue'.[7] On the strength of *Chinua Achebe* and *The Chosen Tongue* – both among the finest studies of their kind – we can ignore the extreme reaction to 'linguistic nationalism'[8] which reaches a point in the occasional attempt to discredit the non-African critic, and direct attention at the more enduring call for the kind of criticism that will recognise and accept the two kinds of contemporary African culture described by Clark as the synthetic or Afro-European and the vernacular-traditional.[9]

Because of the oral medium of much vernacular literary activity it would clearly be hazardous to move from the conventional criticism of written texts to the criticism of traditional vernacular literature without a drastic overhaul of the analytical tools. The call for an African aesthetic is meaningful and non-controversial in this respect. But what I have tried to show so far is that the call for African critical 'concepts', 'standards' or 'criteria' is not a rejection of established modes of literary study like structuralism, neo-Aristotelianism and the like, but a rejection of certain entrenched modes of thinking which perpetuate the stock attitudes to Africa. It has been argued that the cross-cultural transfer of critical methods is an important source of such attitudes. The three solutions recommended are firstly the Marxist approach and the Négritude re-valuations of African culture which I referred to earlier, secondly an open-minded approach which will take the literature on its own terms and use only the internal characteristics of the literary works for critical appraisal, and finally, critical techniques to be evolved by adapting the attitudes and literary patterns abstracted from African folk traditions.

In the second of these solutions the critic is expected to start from a sympathetic position which would enable him to identify the general features of the literature. The common denominator which he finds in the works of the writers will be used as the standard and point of reference for that literature. This is the approach which Larson adopts in *The Emergence of African Fiction* and for which he receives a reviewer's praise for coming so close to finding an African aesthetic.[10] But from the socialist distrust of the Western-educated African which we find in Fanon and Ngugi, to take the writer solely on his own terms would seem unreliable, and the critic requires some training in discrimination to enable him to accept or reject, and to praise or blame. If a literary culture has not a critical tradition in which its critics can be trained, the critic must receive training in an existing tradition elsewhere. The problem here is that although critics in different cultures receive the same kind of (informal) training and discipline in their approach to literature, as distinct from other cultural disciplines like history or agriculture, the question of value depends largely on a cluster of specific needs of culture and era. We must keep this in mind for a just assessment of Larson's achievement.

Stallknecht's Foreword to Larson's book unfortunately puts the reader on his guard:

> African fiction . . . interprets its own world in European terms. . . .
> Tutuola's attitude is undisciplined by a European sense of reality, (p. x)

and

> We are in contact with gifted and sensitive people, now for the first time acquiring or having forced upon them, perhaps rather too suddenly, sophisticated habits of self-observation and self-criticism. . . . Those of us who look with sympathy upon these crises of the spirit will find Dr Larson's exposition a rewarding interpretation. (p. xi)

These phrases alert the reader to some of the assumptions behind Larson's sympathetic criticism, so that the quest for 'Africanisms' seems to betray an over-anxiety to be placed as African in approach. What Larson presents as 'Africanisms' are really the old half-truths about Africa – his ideal Africa is the innocent, traditional Africa of the past which the colonist saw. Larson only drops the condescension for an attitude of acceptance, like using 'anthropological' as a term of praise. His method is therefore not unlike that of Laye who, in *The Radiance of the King*, uses the usual stereotypes about 'primitive' Africa to glorify her in a deliberately ironical manner. But Laye succeeds because his literary use of these stereotypes converts them to metaphors. Larson treats stereotypes as if they were facts. This is an unsafe thing for a critic to do since, by conceptualising the 'Africanisms' which he finds in novels, Larson was preserving these stereotypes. Although Larson acknowledges the danger in using categories, he goes on to apply them. Because of their inflexible character categories have a way of reasserting old stereotypes or creating new ones. Larson does not escape this danger. One can contest every one of his generalisations, even those which offer us useful insights into particular works. Larson argues that 'the most typical narrative form one encounters in contemporary African fiction' (he also stresses that 'actually there is no such thing as a typical African fictional form' (p. 67)) is 'the situational plot' (p. 63). He defines such a plot as one in which the experience presented is 'group felt' and which makes it unnecessary to develop characters in depth.

The view that undeveloped characters are typical of African fiction has been a popular one and was probably first expressed by Professor Abraham of Ghana, who also attributed the phenomenon to the traditional African conception of the individual and society but thought it a shortcoming in written fiction.[11] There is of course a danger in applying to written forms

4

concepts abstracted from the oral tradition. Apart from the communal character of traditional societies, the immediacy of oral communication, which contrasts with the opportunity for meditation that writing offers, must have severely limited the chances of character development in the oral tale. Besides, the oral tale made up for its thin narrative texture with a dramatic vitality, and it is now usually accepted that dramatic characters are not as fully 'rounded' as fictional ones. A too easy reliance on what we know of folklore might lead us into the old fallacies about innocence, simplicity and even to some extent, communalism (were there no absolute monarchies in traditional Africa?).

As Obumselu argues in an essay on changing literary attitudes,[12] African novelists have come to accept the idea of Africa as part of the fallen world. This should lead us to see that *innocence* and *experience* are not very meaningful terms for describing races. When Larson describes *A Grain of Wheat* as appealing to a more Westernised reading audience because of its (Western) psychological complexity (pp. 158–9), he was not only using racial stereotypes, but was also developing a cliché he had mentioned earlier about the novel as an alien form. Are cars and cameras alien to Japan because they were not invented there? It is the inflexibility of critical values which leads directly to the old prejudices about Africa, two of which, time and love, play an important part in Larson's interpretation. We believe that Africans have no interest in time, only in human accomplishments, although markets are held regularly on fixed days, as are naming ceremonies and new yam festivals. Does one need to go further than *Arrow of God* where the appearance of each new moon is awaited with anxiety, to show that time can be valuable in a primarily economic sense? We should allow for the fact that technology and literacy, which bring precision to a society, also partly account for the differences between societies in the degree of precision with which time is reckoned. With their appearance the clock displaces 'sun-up' and 'sun-down'. If we must generalise about human races, we should at least get away from literature to do it, as these two literary/social comments suggest:

Armah's descriptions of physical love are often as graphic as D. H. Lawrence's – most untypical of African writing.
Larson (p. 273)

Here in Africa we do not need a D. H. Lawrence, since – except for a tiny minority who have failed to escape a strict missionary conditioning – there is no horror of sex to be got over on the continent.
David Cook in Heywood's *Perspectives* (p. 145)

5

The most effective thing in Larson's book is the way it brings out very clearly the emerging patterns in African fiction. Also it is clear from the brief last chapter that Larson attempts to get away from his rather fixed way of looking at things. But this does little to change the impression left by the argument of the book, and the work remains disturbing for the way it encourages the reader to see the fiction in terms of standard and non-standard, with an occasional variation in between.

Eustace Palmer's *Introduction to the African Novel* is at first glance less impressive than Larson's book, as it is less ambitious in conception. I think however, that it is less likely to do harm as a work of criticism. Palmer's aims are similar to Larson's. His book even begins with the phrase, 'The emergence of a very large corpus of African novels. . . .' Its approach however contrasts with Larson's. It consists in the discussion of a few key novels in the manner of Kettle's *Introduction to the English Novel*, and is therefore necessarily selective. The omission of *The Interpreters* however seems an unpardonable sin on the part of a writer who expects the ideal novel to possess Kettle's prerequisites of 'life' and 'pattern' or the use of technique to point a moral attitude. Not many African writers come as close to doing this as Soyinka does, although not everyone agrees that the work is wholly successful. This omission, together with other debatable choices like the choice of *No Longer at Ease* rather than *Arrow of God*, show that, to help us determine such issues, we need more comprehensive studies which place African novels in significant relationship with the evolving tradition of fiction.

Margaret Laurence's *Long Drums and Cannons*, may be described as the first attempt at a comprehensive study of a national literature, although it does not include poetry. Mrs Laurence, in spite of her revolutionary approach to the literature through the vernacular tradition, is less interested in literary tradition than in seeking to understand a particular national literature and to relate this to world literature. The lack of continuity between writers in this study makes the idea of a national literature seem an arbitrary thing. What Mrs Laurence is interested in is the extent to which each writer moves through the particularity of his culture to communicate the universals of experience. Her criterion of value is thus not so much the mastery of literary form as the ability of each writer to transcend the specific locale in his work. Thus she says of Nzekwu's *Highlife for Lizards* that it 'does not reach beyond its own time and place' although its dilemmas are 'unquestionably real' within these limits (p. 193).

The study of a national literature might involve a number of emphases, like the relationship of writers to each other and to a common background, the main conventions and trends, as well as the diversity of the literature. Bruce King's *Introduction to Nigerian Literature*, the first real attempt at a comprehensive study of a national literature in Africa reflects the earlier *An Introduction to African Literature* by Ulli Beier in its presentation of oral material not as background or 'influences' but as a more or less independent form. The areas of literature covered belong to three traditions: oral vernacular, vernacular, and English. The King volume thus presents studies of the different local forms and individuals contributing to the growth of a national literature. The method of a collective appreciation of a national literature has been favoured here, and by the *Review of National Literatures* in a recent special number on Black Africa, as a means of avoiding generalisations about the literature. The editorial choice is between concentrating on the unity of each writer's work and seeking to bring out the unity of the literature. The method does not encourage a study of cross-currents or of dominant themes and conventions.

If we turn for example, from the collections by Ulli Beier and Bruce King to Gerald Moore's *The Chosen Tongue* what first becomes apparent is the use of thematic study to provide continuity within the different literatures of an area that is almost as large as that to which Beier introduces us. For the study of such a large area it would be a near impossible feat to relate the work of each writer to its specific background, and we find that Moore discusses the formal features of Yoruba poetry to illustrate Awoonor's experiments whereas the closer source material is the kind of funeral dirges recorded by Professor Nketia.[13] Gerald Moore mentions that Ewe is Awoonor's background. The reason for using a Yoruba illustration, I suppose, is to show the kind of common background from which African poets are working. Moore effectively relates the literature to its background by emphasising the political implications and cultural allusions in many of the works. But it does mean that these allusions have had to be given a literal interpretation in order to bring out the cultural value of the literature.

Adrian Roscoe adopts a more literary approach to interpretation in *Mother is Gold*, a study of Nigerian writing in the context of West African literature and against a background of vernacular literary experience. His analysis of poetry for example is not merely literary but shows an assimilation of material from the cultural background. However Roscoe tends to generalise about the state of literature in the vernacular and its effect on the quality of the works of writers who draw inspiration from it. In spite of its comprehensive approach to the literary area – his study even covers children's literature – the generalisations about the literary background show like some of the works before it that the time has arrived for more studies in depth, and the starting point for this would obviously be monograph studies of individual writers.

Interest in the writer as a person has always been part of literary study.

But apart from the initial interest in the African writer as a special person committed to a national or racial cause, it has often been felt that as the person most aware of the sources of his work, his views and the statement of his intention would throw some light on his work. This is the motive behind the record of the Transcription Centre interviews collected by Duerden and Pieterse in *African Writers Talking*. *Palaver* is a collection of six similar interviews held at Texas by Lindfors and others, and Killam's *African Writers on African Writing* contains essays which provide some insight into the writers' attitudes to life and literature on the continent.

But valuable as these three volumes are they do not tell the whole story of literature. A statement of intention should be only a beginning for the critic, as it was for the writer. Art implies exploration, not the following of a strictly defined path from conception to execution. We must therefore often expect a gap between intention and execution even occasionally in notable cases of a writer's mastery of a particular mode, like Soyinka's well-known ability to stimulate laughter at will in the theatre, or Armah's ability to provoke disgust. Even in these cases where the result apparently conforms to the original plan, our critical curiosity should extend to the way the imagination operates, as a complement to our questions about the writer's intention. *Palaver* gives us an account of the more or less deliberate fashioning of one of Brutus's poems. In spite of this apparent operation of the conscious will in the sometimes deliberate casting round for images in the making of a poem, Brutus places reader and poet on the same level when it comes to appreciating the finished work. This is only saying that intention and effect stand at the poles of creation, and that if the writer allows his original intention to accompany him at the final evaluation he might run the risk of attachment to a position that is no longer relevant or valid. On the other hand, the poem's effect on the reader is relevant to the reader as a means of assessing the final work. It has of course been pointed out that the effect of literature on its audience is unreliable as a criterion for evaluating its worth because of the intrusion of irrelevant personal or stock sentiments in the final evaluation.[14] But then response in a pure form uncontaminated by emotion and sentiment is rarely possible, for this is the channel through which specific values of culture and period get into literary evaluation. Critical evaluation thus depends largely on the effect of literature on the reader; but true critical appreciation is an *ideal* response, and it begins with the discipline which tries to ensure that the reader has been reading well.

In these two forms of response we have the two aesthetic emphases in modern African criticism. The attempt at an objective evaluation belongs to the new university-based criticism. The older affective theory is at the

8

heart of Négritude aesthetics which rejects 'objectivity' and 'disinterested-ness'. Jahn's explanation in *Muntu* that

> every word is an effective word, every word is binding. There is no 'harmless', noncommittal word. (p. 133)

is a gloss on Senghor's theory that 'the beautiful poem is the one which awakens the desired emotion in the public'.[15] In Jahn's discussion of the affective theory he emphasises the therapeutic value of poetry, relating poetry to medicine and drawing support mainly from the status and function of incantatory poetry in traditional societies. The purpose of this affective emphasis is not merely literary – it is not intended as a means of telling the good poem from the bad. We should relate it to the criticism of the Western-educated African with a mind 'largely trained away from our own cultural background',[16] and the demand that literature should be committed to the task of restoring the educated African to a more whole-some mental state.

Commitment implies that literature should not merely exist in a vacuum, with ideas passing from writer to reader, but that the writer, like the reader, should become involved in a kind of ideological dialogue. The importance of a literary traffic of ideas is universally recognised. Frank Kermode points out that 'good reviewing in the weeklies and monthlies is . . . an essential element in the hygiene of a literary culture'.[17] The problem in modern Africa has been that the opportunity for such a dialogue has been scant. What was probably the only vital English medium for such a dialogue was Neogy's *Transition*, and that has become less frequent and less polemical.* The alternative to dialogue in such a form has been the conference of African literature and culture.

Such conferences have produced an important contribution to African criticism. The earliest were from those conferences organised by the Society of African Culture. These have been mainly tied to a programme and broadly based on the arts rather than on literature alone. Emphasis was not on analysis and evaluation but on the elucidation and revaluation of the function and significance of the arts in Africa, as we find in the 1968 *Colloquium on Negro Art*. Anglophone conferences were less streamlined to a programme (Okigbo once described one of these as a jamboree).[18] For example, no single theme or attitude dominates the Ife Conference of 1968 represented in Heywood's *Perspectives on African Literature*.[19] The unwillingness to be held down to a position is what separates the English temper from the French on the continent. Thus in the only collection of essays in English written to a single, premeditated theme, *Protest and*

* *Transition* is now edited by Wole Soyinka (Ed.).

9

Conflict in African Literature, the editors point out that 'there are dangers in analysing works of literature within the confines of a single theme' while accepting the validity and logic of choosing that particular theme (p. x).

In spite of this apparently impassable gulf of differences in attitudes to criticism, Francophone and Anglophone Africa are united in identifying a common problem and in prescribing a common remedy. This is the reason for the joint publication of the papers of the Conferences held at the University of Dakar and Fourah Bay College, Freetown as *African Literature and the Universities* and published, appropriately, at the Ibadan University Press. The problem is that of an appropriate African audience for African literature. Its importance is shown by Achebe's half-serious remark that the African intellectual reads nothing,[20] thus indirectly affirming the persistence of a situation described nearly two decades earlier by Nwikina, a Nigerian librarian: 'The new literate [Nigerian] does not read books, because he has not been trained to read books', and 'as a rule the Nigerian reads for a purpose'.[21]

Since Nwikina mentions the role of Onitsha publishers in feeding a semi-literate audience with literary material, it would seem that the problem then as now was seen primarily as a middle-class problem. Besides the solution was believed to lie with the universities. The importance of an academic tradition of criticism was stressed by critic after critic, as we find, for example, in 'The African Writer and His Public' by Mohamadou Kane,[22] and in the rejection of Nkrumah's indictment of the universities by Pieterse and Munro who insist on the importance of universities for keeping a literary culture alive.[23]

Lest this be thought a desperate defence of the ivory tower by academics under siege, it is necessary to show, from Gerald Moore's introduction to *African Literature and the Universities*, that the kind of hope placed on the work of African universities, was that through them 'the revolutionary idea of teaching young Africans about Africa might even percolate down to the primary level' (p. 1). In other words, the work of criticism is primarily an educational one. The primary audience consists of undergraduates who, on graduation, reach down to the lower levels through secondary school teaching and radio reviewing, as at present in Nigeria.

In a partially spontaneous response to this need there have arisen journals to cater for the various critical needs such as explication (*African Literature Today*), experiments with a particular kind of analysis (*The Conch*), and reports of research in progress (*Research in African Literatures*). The first fruits of the techniques favoured by these journals are present in two monographs by the editors of the first two of these journals, Jones's *The Writing of Wole Soyinka* and Anozie's *Christopher Okigbo*.

10

The monograph is a more specialised form of criticism than the general survey because it combines factual material, especially biography, with analysis and evaluation. The current popularity of critical monographs (there are at least nine at the time of writing and all by university teachers) shows that the responsibility for shaping an African tradition of criticism has passed from its Négritude home to the academy. Thus, although the African publishers of *Whispers from a Continent* describe it as an essential point of departure for subsequent criticism, it is more like the high watermark of Négritude philosophy, a fully mature, rather than a seminal work. In spite of the very personal character of its response, the critic's remarkable talent for responding to sounds and for linking man with nature on the continent suggests Négritude philosophy as its antecedent. In fact the chapter on Négritude is the most inspired in the book. Cartey's book is almost a justification for the continued tolerance of the affective view of literature, although one might object to its method – a procrustean arrangement of themes in a sequence that harmonises with the political history of Africa, as we find also in Shelton's anthology and part of Larson's history of African fiction.[24] The affective warmth of Cartey's response reaches us through his ability to listen to and interpret the sounds of the literature. He thus manages to communicate to the reader his strong awareness of the trauma of colonialism.

The affective approach appears in a more innocuous form in Theroux's essay on Okigbo.[25] It disarms objection because it has been 'smuggled' into the academic tradition through the back-door of a popular approach to teaching children. In this method of pedagogy pitched in a low key Theroux recommends that we listen and surrender to the affective power of Okigbo's sounds before seeking to understand.

Published only a year after the essay by Theroux, Anozie's *Christopher Okigbo* recommends an approach that contrasts with Theroux's. Anozie maintains a balance of praise and censure in his personal portrait of Okigbo, although one might almost catch an occasional whiff of bardolatry coming through the character sketch. Yet as far as Anozie's critical approach is concerned, feeling is suspect, as he makes clear in this description of the structuralist approach as

> simply a way of feeling (a true structuralist student would, by the way, frown at the emotive word) one's way through any given dense system of codes or symbolic relationships. (p. 156)

Because the subject is seen mainly as a system of codes, the method is not allowed to become an exercise in pure formalism, and there is a constant harking back to the sociological background of the work being discussed. Also we do get the impression now and then that literature is becoming at best only a means of inquiry into the nature of imagination. It is true that Anozie reins in his metaphysical horse by relegating his philosophical models to the status of mere analogy, but he occasionally admits that the method does not always suit the character of literature:

> Okigbo in *Limits* II is not interested in any doctrinal philosophy. The poem itself seems very ill at ease when we try to see it within the framework of a systematized principle of life. (p. 76)

Therefore, for me, the most illuminating sections include those straight critical appreciations unclogged by philosophical discourse, like the discussion of *Limits* III, surely one of the most lucid in the book.

The most impressive section of the book however, is the 'Structural Approach to Distances' in which Anozie applies the structural method with a consistency unequalled elsewhere in the book, and a disciplined exclusion of the usual sociological asides. The application of the method here recommends itself as an effective means of unravelling 'any given dense system of codes', and it has a further attraction as a defence against a merely impressionistic view of a poem. But there are a few chinks in this splendid armour. Its most important weakness has been caused by the critic himself. For some unexplained reason he sticks to an early version of the texts in an almost total neglect of the *Labyrinths* version which Okigbo described as 'somewhat different and . . . final'. The reason is probably the critic's interest in using Okigbo's sources, since Anozie utilises almost as many references as Okigbo borrowed phrases. But by so limiting the relevance of his work for an accurate understanding of the *Labyrinths* poems, Anozie seems to attach no very great importance to revision as a means of discovering or creating *new* meaning through an exploration or manipulation of language. For example, in his reading of 'Silent Sisters' he interprets the line,

No wrinkles on the salt face of glass

as an image of the sea's impartiality and its function as preserver, whereas in the *Labyrinths* version Okigbo substitutes the opposite image,

More wrinkles on the salt face of glass.

In both versions, the source of fear is not the sea itself, but the wild winds which cry out against the sisters and disturb the sea's face. In the altered version, however, the sisters' hope comes not from the sea's face, but from pure faith, since the sea's face is at least disturbed by the wild winds.

By this deliberate use of the first rather than the final version of the poems, Anozie ignores one logical implication of his method. The internal

12

coherence or self-sufficiency of poems which lend themselves to structural analysis renders early authorial intentions irrelevant and makes early versions of less value than final ones. With such internal coherence we may assume the non-existence of God within the universe he has created. This was what Okigbo meant by saying he did not write the 'Lament of the Drums', but only created the drums which then said what they liked.[26] Anozie has coined an excellent name for it – 'Okigbo's poetic "ventriloquism".'[27] Given its logical extension, as Anozie often does, such ventriloquism forces the reader to seek within the work itself for its meaning and its values. This is why Anozie argues that it is not really just to rely mainly on 'content' – that attractive lodestone of criticism – for getting at the 'meaning' of a work as most critics do, even if it does lead them to the goal.[28] The true *meaning* must be sought for in the totality of its tone, form as well as 'content' (another version of the 'significant form' of formalist critics?).

We may apply this principle of meaning to the last line of *Limits* ('And the cancelling out is complete'), described by Anozie as 'an impertinent error', and ask whether 'cancelling out' is properly related to the rest of the poem. To cancel out, in the idiom of the poem, is to get even. It is a poetic image drawn from arithmetic in which one arrives at an irreducible fraction by cancellation. The eagles had earlier killed the sunbird and divided the ornaments, etc. of the twin gods of the forest, and it is these acts which the sunbird is now triumphantly cancelling out. If properly listened to and intuitively received, this line has a rightness about it because of the echoes which link it with similar sounds in earlier lines. From this it would be seen that in addition to offering insight into his use of sources, Anozie's academic technique is valuable mainly as a supplement to the kind of intuitive response which Theroux recommends. It helps to uncover meaning but mainly as a post-response check on impressionism.

In Eldred Jones's *The Writing of Wole Soyinka* we come to a method which seeks an objective technique without totally eliminating feeling and ordinary response, and which is accessible to various levels of the audience. Jones relies on attention to image patterns and shifts of tense in a way which occasionally recalls the style of the New Critics. In this respect the study differs from the sociological criticism of Gerald Moore's parallel study, *Wole Soyinka*. An even more clearly marked difference is Jones's complete reliance on the power of intuition and analysis to tease meaning from the words on the page without any reference to author's intention. Unlike Moore, whose chief purpose is to relate a literary work to its cultural and intellectual sources as well as the life of the writer, Jones would rather trust the tale and not the teller, as Lawrence once recommended.

13

Thus, Soyinka's works are treated more as literary works having similar properties with literary works elsewhere than as signposts to contemporary African Culture, as in Moore. Again and again we come across the tabooed word 'universal', used even for items which Larson would have labelled 'Africanisms'. Thus Forest Father, an English rendering of Yoruba *Olu igbo* (Lord of the Forest), is described by Jones as 'the Yoruba *style* deity' (italics mine), while he says of Soyinka's characters, 'Man is dressed for the nonce in African dress' (p. 11).

This position has two major implications for literary study and literature teaching. First, greater attention is paid to the integrity of the literary work, which is seen in an Aristotelian manner as a microcosm. Secondly, it raises the question, how values of a non-formal kind may enter into critical appreciation without shattering the implied integrity of the work. These two problems are considered in Jones's attitude to Soyinka's writing. His denial of the ability of poetry to save the world (p. 152) is a rejection of the usual faith in the practical value of the arts in Africa. It does not however lead him into a purely formal position, for he also sees a civilising influence in Soyinka's work. These two sides of Jones's position leads one to ask how civilising influences may be determined by means of a technique which distrusts overt didacticism. For does not Jones devalue a poem like 'In Memory of Segun Awolowo' in which Soyinka rationalises the experience? One solution is to see the literary work as a dramatic creation which permits the effacement of its author. The reader is not merely thrown back on his own moral resources but is offered guides to judgement, like the use of irony and other deflationary devices. For example, in spite of the monstrous character of Kongi which nearly splits the play into the poles of good and evil, Kongi's enemies are not to be taken completely on their own terms because Soyinka exposes their weaknesses by the use of irony, as we find when the excuse in Sarumi's song betrays the oppressive luxury in which the traditional obas lived before Kongi:

> Oh yes, we know they say
> We wore out looms
> With weaving robes for kings
> But I ask, is *popoki* [thick coarse cloth]
> The stuff to let down
> To unformed fingers clutching up
> At life? (*Kongi's Harvest*, pp. 8–9)

The emphasis on the poem *per se* is meant not only to prevent the reader from being led away by irrelevant associations from what is actually in the poem, but also to nurture a student's sensibility to poetry and equip him

14

to appreciate not only the familiar and well-annotated poem, but also the unfamiliar – a point which I. A. Richards makes in *Practical Criticism*. The method is not foolproof, of course, and it would be naive to use it always with a total disregard for some of the sources of poetry. Eldred Jones has an introductory chapter which he calls 'Man and background', and which is equivalent in a general way to the background of biography, social history, and Yoruba culture in Gerald Moore's book. A poem like 'In Memory of Segun Awolowo' shows that one cannot always disregard the sources of a work. A teacher would be hard put to it explaining the meaning of the lines

drove
The last flint deepest
In the heart of patience

to an inquisitive student without going outside the poem to refer to the extra trials which this death has brought to Segun's already suffering parent.

What Gerald Moore seeks to achieve in *Wole Soyinka* is the insight which the use of background gives. As a result of this emphasis the book is only a little more than a background for Soyinka's work. The Moore who writes in *Wole Soyinka* is not the Moore of *Seven African Writers* but the Moore of those cultural essays, 'Time and Experience in African Poetry' and 'The Imagery of Death in African Poetry'.[29] The gradual shift from literary to essentially social values can be seen, for example, in the criterion which he employs for evaluating the merits of Soyinka's poem, 'Malediction': he criticises in it 'an excess of hatred as ugly as the emotion [which Soyinka] attacks' (p. 96), rather than its turgidity, a quality which Moore finds also in the Nirvana sleep-walkers stanza of 'Idanre'.

What Moore apparently distrusts however is not literary appreciation – he is still a reliable guide to literary quality – but literary analysis, or the exposure of the inner secrets of a literary work. His exposition of *A Dance of the Forests* closes with a remark about the 'exceptional impenetrability' of Demoke's final speech. The speech can of course be deciphered by the ordinary method of critical analysis once it has been recognised that it is in the incantatory form of oral literature. Its unstated allusions hint at the endless conflict between Sango and Ogun and the need for earthing which Demoke, Ogun's protegé, has come to acknowledge. The speech is of course impenetrable on stage. This is the justification for Moore's position – his respect for the genre. Moore first expressed distrust for academic analysis and its threat to the sanctity of art in his introduction to *African Literature and the Universities* (p. 4).

The development of the kind of criticism which Moore objected to has led to the loss of the kind of lyricism one finds in the Négritude style which is present I believe in Senghor's rhetorical essays and to some extent in Cartey's lyrical appreciation. In contrast the uninspired plot summaries which we sometimes encounter in academic criticism are often needed for analysis. The supremacy of academic analysis lies however in its precision and the persuasive logic of its conclusions. Afolayan's argument about the Yoruba source of Tutuola's prose rhythms[30] does little more than provide scientific documentation and validation for Jahn's theory of the neo-African style, although Jahn's speculative approach makes his statements far less persuasive. This paradox shows what criticism should do to find acceptance in an age of science, just as Anozie's method, which at times becomes 'futuristic' by assimilating itself into mathematics, shows perhaps how far criticism should go to find this acceptance.

In fairness to the evolving academic tradition in Africa, it should be admitted that critics have generally resisted the divorce of literature from life even when their practice is at its most formal. This may be explained, not by the insistence that there is no 'art for art's sake' in Africa – really a case of crying wolf when there is none, since pleasure itself is an artistic function – but by the present intellectual climate which encourages the critical faculty described by Irele as the sociological imagination.[31] The political option implied in this preference for sociological significance over moral values may be related to the precedence which political liberation takes over religious piety in Africa. This alone alleviates the injustice of the attacks on the moral zeal of African satirists on political grounds. I am thinking in particular of criticisms of Soyinka (from whose work the theme of colonialism is almost completely absent – it is absent from even his independence play, *A Dance of the Forests*), and Armah. Two essays which seem comparatively mild but whose patriotism seems to me misplaced are Ngugi's essay on Nigerian satirists,[32] and Aidoo's review of *The Beautyful Ones Are Not Yet Born*.[33] The artistic compassion which we find in a work like *A Grain of Wheat*, admirable though it is, is no substitute for satire. In spite of its apparently unpatriotic attack on the artist's own people satire has a sociological value too – it possesses the literary virtue of attempting to exorcise evil by calling its name. The question of the selective distortion of history can be met by Aristotle's distinction between history, as a record of things that did happen, and literature as a creation of things that are probable and could happen. The satirist seeks to warn by creating particular (African) instances of probable situations, and he deserves tolerance.

The orientation of criticism towards sociology has produced one positive model of tolerance in the sympathetic studies of the popular

16

literary culture of Onitsha.[34] Such tolerance has been denied related literature at higher levels, which cannot bear the close scrutiny applied in serious literary study.[35] Such a strict standard is necessary as a means of encouraging the right reading of literature and training the reader to uncover the stock attitudes behind cliché and other dead language forms. One of the functions of criticism is thus to encourage the right reading of literature as a weapon against indoctrination and the habituating of people to a certain mode of behaviour through propaganda, as Soyinka has pointed out.[36] But we must stop at this point: The next step may lead to the false position that our salvation lies in the right reading of literature.

The functions of criticism to literature, audience, and society are legion. In all cases some consideration for the text is essential; but no single critical orientation can be adequate. The best we can do is to discourage the complacency of simple attitudes and the tyranny of uniformity.

NOTES

1. Full references for primary works of criticism are given in the bibliography. Page references appear in the text.
2. 'Where Angels Fear to Tread' in Killam (1973), pp. 4–7.
3. 'African Literature' in *Présence Africaine*, Eng. ed., xx, 48, 1963, p. 49.
4. J. F. A. Ajayi, 'The Continuity of African Institutions Under Colonialism' in *Emerging Themes of African History*, ed. T. O. Ranger (Nairobi, East African Publishing House, 1968), pp. 189–200.
5. Ngugi, 'The African Writer and His Past' in Heywood, p. 3; Achebe, 'Interview with Chinua Achebe' in Lindfors, *et al.*, pp. 5–6.
6. Abiola Irele, 'The Criticism of Modern African Literature' in Heywood, *Perspectives*, p. 21.
7. The idea first occurs in Moore's *Seven African Writers*, p. vii.
8. The phrase is from S. O. Anozie's review of *The Chosen Tongue* in *The Conch*, II, i, 1970, p. 69.
9. 'Interview with John Pepper Clark' in Lindfors, *et. al.*, p. 16.
10. 'Through the Drum', *Times Literary Supplement*, 29 December 1972, p. 1573.
11. *Mind of Africa*, pp. 96–7.
12. Ben Obumselu, 'African Eden: Cultural Nationalism in the African Novel' in *Ibadan Studies in English*, II, 1, June 1970, pp. 131–55.
13. Nketia, *Funeral Dirges of the Akan People* (Achimota, 1955).

14. See I. A. Richards, *Practical Criticism* (London, Routledge & Kegan Paul, 1964), pp. 235–54.
15. *Senghor: Prose and Poetry*, selected and translated by John Reed and Clive Wake (London, O.U.P., 1965), p. 83.
16. Abiola Irele in Heywood, *Perspectives*, p. 21.
17. Frank Kermode, *Modern Essays* (London, Fontana, 1970), p. 125.
18. 'Transition Conference Questionnaire', *Transition*, II, 5, July–August 1962, p. 12.
19. For a summary of the discussions at the Conference see *Journal of the Nigerian English Studies Association*, II, 2, 1968, pp. 143–78.
20. 'What Do African Intellectuals Read?', *Times Literary Supplement*, 12 May 1972, p. 547.
21. Gbole H. Nwikina, 'Books in the Battle for Learning', *West African Review*, xxv, 316, January 1954, pp. 44–5.
22. This essay was published by Mohamadou Kane in *Présence Africaine*, Eng. ed., xxx, 58, 1966, pp. 10–32, but was erroneously attributed to Cheikh Hamidou Kane the novelist, in Killam, 1973, pp. 53–72.
23. *Protest and Conflict*, p. xii.
24. Austin Shelton, *The African Assertion: a critical anthology of African literature* (New York, Odyssey Press, 1968), cf. Larson, p. 114.
25. In King, pp. 135–51.
26. Interview with Serumaga in Duerden and Pieterse, p. 143.
27. *Christopher Okigbo*, p. 120.
28. *Christopher Okigbo*, p. 83 *n.*
29. Gerald Moore, 'Time and Experience in African Poetry', *Transition*, VI, 26, 1966, pp. 18–22; and 'The Imagery of Death in African Poetry', *Africa*, xxxviii, 1, 1968, pp. 57–70.
30. A. Afolayan, 'Language and Sources of Amos Tutuola' in Heywood, pp. 49–63.
31. In Heywood, p. 17.
32. Ngugi, 'Satire in Nigeria' in Pieterse and Munro, pp. 56–69.
33. Aidoo, 'Our Saviours' in Killam, 1973, pp. 14–18.
34. Emmanuel Obiechina, *An African Popular Literature*, London, C.U.P., 1973), to name an important example.
35. Cf. Palmer's reason for excluding Ekwensi from his study of 'masters of African fiction': 'Ekwensi also mars his work by vulgarising his style to suit the needs of a mass audience'. *An Introduction to the African Novel*, p. xi.
36. Wole Soyinka, 'The Choice and Use of Language' in *Cultural Events in Africa*, No. 75, 1971, p. 4.

Bibliography

W. E. Abraham, *The Mind of Africa* (London, Weidenfeld and Nicolson, 1967).
Sunday O. Anozie, *Christopher Okigbo* (London, Evans; New York, Africana, 1972).
Ulli Beier, ed., *Introduction to African Literature* (London, Longmans, 1964).
David Carroll, *Chinua Achebe* (New York, Twayne, 1970).
Wilfred Cartey, *Whispers from a Continent* (London, Heinemann, 1971).

*J. P. Clark, *The Example of Shakespeare* (London, Longman, 1970).
*Harold R. Collins, *Amos Tutuola* (New York, Twayne, 1969).
Dennis Duerden and Cosmo Pieterse, eds., *African Writers Talking* (London, Heinemann; New York, Africana, 1972).
Frantz Fanon, *The Wretched of the Earth* (London, Penguin, 1969).
Albert S. Gerard, ed., *Review of National Literatures*, II, 2 (Fall 1971): *Black Africa*.
Christopher Heywood, ed., *Perspectives on African Literature* (London, Heinemann; New York, Africana, 1971).
Janheinz Jahn, *A History of Neo-African Literature* (London, Faber, 1966).
Muntu: an Outline of Neo-African Culture (London, Faber, 1958).
Eldred Durosimi Jones, *The Writing of Wole Soyinka* (London, Heinemann, 1973).
G. D. Killam, *African Writers on African Writing* (London, Heinemann, 1973).
The Novels of Chinua Achebe (London, Heinemann; New York, Africana, 1969).
Bruce King, ed., *Introduction to Nigerian Literature* (London and Lagos, University of Lagos and Evans; New York, Africana, 1971).
Charles R. Larson, *The Emergence of African Fiction* (London, Bloomington, Indiana University Press, 1971).
Margaret Laurence, *Long Drums and Cannons* (London, Macmillan, 1968).
Bernth Lindfors, et al., *Palaver: Interviews with Five African Writers in Texas* (Austin, Texas, African and Afro-American Institute, 1972).
Taban lo Liyong, *The Last Word* (Nairobi, East Africa Publishing Co., 1969).
Gerald Moore, ed., *African Literature and the Universities* (Ibadan, Ibadan University Press, 1965).
Gerald Moore, *The Chosen Tongue* (London, Longman, 1969).
Seven African Writers (London, O.U.P., 1962).
Wole Soyinka (London, Evans; New York, Africana, 1971).
Ezekiel Mphahlele, *The African Image* (London, Faber, 1962).
Emmanuel Obiechina, *An African Popular Literature* (London, Cambridge University Press, 1973).
Eustace Palmer, *An Introduction to the African Novel* (London, Heinemann; New York, Africana, 1972).
Cosmo Pieterse and Donald Munro, eds., *Protest and Conflict in African Literature* (London, Heinemann, 1969).
Arthur Ravenscroft, *Chinua Achebe* (London, Longmans; New York, Africana, 1969).
Adrian A. Roscoe, *Mother is Gold* (London, Cambridge University Press, 1971).
Society of African Culture: *Colloquium on Negro Art* (1st World Festival of Negro Arts), *Présence Africaine*, 1968.
Martin Tucker, *Africa in Modern Literature* (New York, Frederick Ungar, 1971).
Ngugi Wa Thiong'o, *Homecoming* (London, Heinemann, 1972).
Michael Wade, *Peter Abrahams* (London, Evans, 1971).
Paer Wästberg, ed., *The Writer in Modern Africa* (Uppsala, The Scandinavian Institute of African Studies; New York, Africana, 1968).

* Starred works are not referred to.

African Critics
on African Literature:
A Study in Misplaced Hostility

Solomon Ogbede Iyasere

Remarkable in the development of African literature is the intensity with which African critics have become engaged in the criticism and review of African creative works. The significance of this development cannot be overemphasised: it provides a diversity in the critical responses to African literature and will end the dominance by the Western voices in the criticism of African literature. The danger inherent in this domination by non-Africans has been pointed out by Eldred Jones. At the Seminar on African Literature and the University Curriculum held at Fourah Bay in April 1963, Jones argues, 'When the main critical voices are non-African there is a danger that the writers may come to emphasise the values which they think their foreign readership demands. This could lead to an expatriate literature produced by Africans, and to false artistic values'.[1]

Jones' view, which is still popular among perceptive African critics, seems to derive in most part from the observation that the majority of Western critics emphasise non-literary elements in African creative writings, especially in the earlier novels – the socio-anthropological details, the quaint, and, to them, the exotic aspects. They ignore how these writers strive, if with mixed success, to use language to translate and transform their vision of social reality into perceivable form. And, it seems that as a result of this disproportionate interest in the 'curiosities' of African culture that a number of less than second-rate novels, works of little or no literary quality – Ekwensi's *Jagua Nana*, Aluko's *One Man, One Wife*, and Nzekwu's *Wand of Noble Wood*, to cite but a few of the more prominent failures – received blanket critical acclaim from the Western liberal chic.

Given this situation, many African critics and authors agree with Jones' protest against the Western views but do not always assent to his reason for doing so. 'Engaged' African critics see Western domination as but another form of neo-colonialism, and often object as well to the use of Western critical standards. For example, the editors of *Présence Africaine* have expressed the opinion, 'The soul of our people will not be heard in the concert of nations until they have regained their artists, their authority to judge and their privileges as consumers and interpreters of their works of art. In short they must retrieve the organic dimensions of their own vitality. . . .'[2] More blatantly, Joseph Okpaku insists, 'The primary criticism of African art must come from Africans using African standards. We cannot accept either of the two existing approaches to criticism of African literature. It is as undesirable to plead for leniency in criticising African works as it is absurd for Lewis Nkosi to ask that Western critical standards be used.'[3] According to these views, African literature belongs to Africans alone and not to the public, and only Africans using undefined African standards can validly and judiciously evaluate African creative works.

Yet judging from the increasing criticism of African literature by Africans, we Africans ourselves – with all our so-called 'inside knowledge' of the social realities behind the novels at our disposal – have not provided significantly more insightful criticism. In most cases, as this paper will argue, responses are too often apologetic defences of mediocre works with a vehement display of misplaced hostility towards anyone – and especially towards the Western critic – who dares see faults in the contemporary novelists. In our developing criticism as in our developing literature we seem as yet uncertain as to what issues are of prime importance. This uncertainty is perhaps the reason for the excessive concerns we – like the Westerners we seek to repudiate – exhibit for dubious questions seldom of literary significance. For surely to argue which critic is 'more African' and can produce the 'more African' criticism takes us far afield from any meaningful evaluation of the work itself. Clearly African fiction, as Derek Elders rightly points out in his review of *The Novels of Chinua Achebe* by G. D. Killam, still largely interests by its treatment of matter peripheral to the intrinsically literary: by what they are about rather than what they are as works of art. Startlingly, we African critics who are supposed to elevate the criticism of African literature to a higher degree of literary excellence and help explain those 'curious African features' that seem to baffle the aesthetic sensibilities of the Western critics, are now ironically engaged in the bardolatry criticism that Killam and Judith Gleason have made famous.

This mode of criticism, a corruption of the critical which illuminates more about the critic's idiosyncrasies than the work examined, is exhibited in its crass form in Ernest Emenyonu's recent essay, 'African Literature: What Does It Take To Be Its Critic?', in *African Literature Today*, Volume 5. Focusing on the now belaboured issue, the inability of Western critics to criticise African creative works perceptively 'because of their profound lack of knowledge about African cultural traditions coupled with an ignorance of the existence, nature, and depth of the heritage of the African oral tradition',[4] Emenyonu concentrates on the criticism of Ekwensi by Bernth Lindfors. Emenyonu castigates Lindfors for describing Ekwensi's art of fiction in the following terms:

> At least nine novels, four of them still unpublished, six novelettes for school children, two collections of folktales and dozens of short stories have poured forth from his pen, but not one is entirely free of amateurish blots and blunders, not one could be called the handiwork of a careful and skilled craftsman. Ekwensi may be simply too impatient an artist to take pains with his work or to learn by a calm rational process of trial and error. When he is not repeating his old mistakes, he is stumbling upon spectacular new ones. As a consequence, many of his stories and novels serve as excellent examples of how not to write fiction.[5]

The most crucial and most damaging of Lindfors' comments are those which deal with Ekwensi's craft of fiction – that Ekwensi is not only a mediocre writer, but one who is constitutionally unable to master the art of fiction. It is not the social realities that Ekwensi perceives that is at issue here, nor even the chief factors that have influenced Ekwensi's portrayal of these realities, as Emenyonu struggles to make us believe, but the irrefutable fact that Ekwensi fails to explore and render that perception into a significant, coherent whole.

Yet, in his defence of Ekwensi, Emenyonu places unqualified emphasis on peripheral matters, matters of little or no literary importance. In fact, nowhere in his essay does Emenyonu come to terms with the crux of the problem. Instead of defending Ekwensi's artistic integrity (if indeed Ekwensi ever had any) against Lindfors, as he proposes to do, Emenyonu gives us an extended 'biographical history' of Ekwensi's life and restates Ekwensi's socio-political beliefs:

> Ekwensi believes that although 'politics awaken similar trends of thought in all peoples, its approach by an African is not necessarily the same as that of the American or Irish'. The writer must discover this element of psychology which is inherent in the behavior of the Africans and bring this out when he writes. The psychological characteristic is always present in the African in whatever creative situation he is placed whether in a historical, political or romantic novel. When a writer succeeds in portraying this authentic picture of the African and his setting, if none other, at least Africans themselves will recognize it. . . .
> In spite of what Lindfors thinks is Ekwensi's motive for writing *Jagua Nana* it must be said that the theme of his novels is in keeping with Ekwensi's stated involvement with African cities undergoing tremors of transition.

But this is not the point. What Ekwensi believes in personally or what he professes to be his mission in life or his socio-political design is his own affair. What we literary critics (African or non-African) must judge him by is not what he believes, but what he sets before us; not what he sees, but how effectively he renders his particular vision. 'Intention as intention will not do the trick; intention has to be joined by skill. A man might intend a fine saw and make a botch of it.'[6]

Emenyonu, like Oladele Taiwo, is simply blind to such an important distinction, as he is blind to the distinction between art and reality, artistic rendition and photographic reproduction. This inability to perceive these crucial differences comes through in Emenyonu's assertion, 'When a writer succeeds in portraying this *authentic picture* of the African and his setting, if none other, at least Africans themselves will recognise it.' (emphasis mine) And, while decrying the 'sound and fury' which 'signify nothing' in the Western critics Lindfors and Austin J. Shelton, Emenyonu has done little better himself. He denigrates Lindfors' effort to assign to Western influences some of the weaknesses of Ekwensi's work but responds to only half of the issue. Emenyonu claims that Ekwensi has not been so influenced by Western novels as he has by his Nigerian upbringing and then insists that Lindfors' assessment of Ekwensi is wrong because of his failure to acknowledge the importance of Ekwensi's African background. But this argument over influences does not vindicate Ekwensi nor give us any reason to see Ekwensi as a talented writer. Ironically, all Emenyonu has done is to disparage Ekwensi's Nigerian cultural heritage by un-wittingly laying at its doorstep the blame for Ekwensi's mediocrity. Once this act is recognised, Lindfors' charges against Ekwensi still stand. And justifiably so. While I do not agree with their critical methods, I find I must join Lindfors and Eustace Palmer[7] in pointing out the shortcomings of Ekwensi, a writer I elsewhere described as one 'hired to depress art'.[8]

We Africans must be sympathetic and encouraging to our writers but we must not allow our patriotic zeal to blind us to their faults. Indeed, it is our duty to point them out where they occur. It is only through sensitive and informed criticism that we can establish a healthy tradition of criticism of African literature. Even Achebe's efforts are not always successful and Ekwensi does not stand with Achebe, just as Achebe does not stand with Soyinka or Clark. To praise all is to praise none. We cannot shrink from an honest evaluation of our writers nor eliminate as 'un-African' any formal aspects of the novel at which a writer may not be successful. For example, to accept Abiola Irele's well-intentioned though misguided proposal that 'eoherence' should not be one of the criteria for the evaluation of African creative works is to underrate both the achievement and the potential of our writers. We must not castrate in the name of 'Africanism' the literature we cherish.

As if over-sensitive to any statement that our writers are less than perfect, we have become too quick to criticise – and even attempt to maul – those critics, especially Westerners, who find fault with our authors. I am not saying that we should not correct those who have criticised wrongly, but we must do so on literary, that is, textual grounds, not patriotic or racial ones. As we must condemn such Western critics who engage in 'gratuitous paternalistic criticism', and employ their own cultural idiosyncrasies in evaluating African fiction, so we must also condemn those of us who use literary criticism as a 'viaticum' for protesting colonial and neo-colonial abuses, no matter how justifiable our case may be. Differences in judgement on a work are not settled by name-calling, nor by consulting the Ifa oracle, nor yet by private conversations with the author – but only by turning directly to the text itself. We must examine closely what the writer has set before us and the terms in which he embodies his perceptions. If the work cannot stand by itself, for itself, then no amount of cultural apprenticeship nor narcissistic indulgence can defend it. Unless we do shift our focus to the work itself, we will be as guilty as the Western critics of over-emphasising the non-literary aspects. In our criticism we, too, often fail to distinguish between factual content and mode of expression. Because we are Africans we assume we have essential 'inside knowledge' about the social realities behind the creative works. At the same time, we may fail, as do Emenyonu and Taiwo, to distinguish between reality and art. Whatever the reason, we have become overly concerned with the socio-cultural and traditional aspects of the works and then use this information as the basis for evaluation without considering how these elements function. Rarely do we examine the artistic aspects: how these socio-cultural realities are transformed into art. An example may be afforded by E. Ofori Akyea's recent study, 'Traditionalism in African Literature: J. P. Clark'.[9] In this essay, Akyea catalogues those traditional Ijaw elements, such as proverbs and stories about the heaven and the earth, which are present in Clark's *Ozidi*. On the basis of these elements of tradition, some of which are similar to those of Akyea's own people, the Ewes, Akyea then asserts that *Ozidi* is a successful work of art. While it is almost a truism that Clark's *Ozidi* is a fine piece, its success and its beauty derive not simply from the fact that Clark draws upon the traditional, but that he uses these elements to serve a deliberate artistic purpose. But Akyea does not show us how these traditional elements function to advance the meaning and intensify the power of Clark's drama. It is not sufficient to know only that these elements are traditional. We must know as well what these elements contribute to the work in order to judge Clark's artistry and discretion in

24

using them. Do they add the appeal of the familiar, or the dignity of ritual, or the mystery of ceremony? Do they define the setting or provide insight into character? Are they a source of unity and order? In other words, what is their function? How do they work? Akyea does not discuss these crucial matters. He labels the traditional but does no more. Yet any literary criticism worthy of the name must show not only *what* but also *how*.

It may be argued that since most African writers present their perceptions discursively, with extensive authorial comment, or attempt to use their works as storehouses of petrified ethnographic 'truths', this form of criticism which emphasises the anthropological and socio-cultural data is valid. Shelton calls for a form of this criticism: 'African literature, indeed, reflects African values. . . . The European might use any of numerous critical techniques, singly or in combination, but most of them will not lead him any closer to the truth than guess work might. Each requires some knowledge of the African writer's cultural background not merely study of text alone.'[10] And we Africans seem to have seized upon this mode of criticism, insisting we have this additional information – as Emenyonu claims to have about Ekwensi – and perhaps some kind of inherited insight that will make us better critics of African authors. In practice, we critics do what Nzekwu does as a novelist. We use a work as he uses a situation in a novel: as a jumping-off place for an exhibition of our knowledge of African customs and traditions – our 'Africanism'. 'How African we are!' we seem to say, peddling our cultural heritage in much the same way that Benin bronzes are peddled in New York or Paris. But this method will work no better for us critics than it works for Nzekwu. Perhaps we cannot discard altogether extra-textual explanations, for we must be informed as well as sensitive. But what 'knowledge of the African writer's cultural background' or discussions of traditional practices, are brought in must always serve the end of illuminating what the work itself presents. We must not allow ourselves the exhibitionism of which Nzekwu is guilty. And we cannot expect that because we are Africans our explanations will necessarily be better than those of a scholar-critic who is not. Here the distinction between criticism and pre-criticism must be borne in mind. The information about cultural backgrounds is simply information, descriptive and not evaluative. Of itself, it does not elucidate the work. As information, it can be ascertained by any careful study. But when we apply this information as an aid in explicating a text, we move from the descriptive to the analytical and evaluative and it is here that the literary critic's task begins. Many African critics, especially the ancestralists, do not make this distinction between pre-criticism and criticism. For this reason, there exists a confusion between the two and a strong tendency to pass off socio-anthropological commentary as literary criticism.

Indeed, most of what has been published under the rubric 'literary criticism' is precisely this type of socio-anthropological commentary. Novels in which social and political realities are discursively presented and obtusely elaborated by the author – Nwapa's *Efuru* and *Idu*, Achebe's *A Man of the People*, or the novels mentioned at the beginning of this essay – enjoy frequent attention from Africans as well as from Westerners. On the other hand, Soyinka's *The Interpreters*, Okara's *The Voice*, or Awoonor's *This Earth, My Brother* arouse significantly less interest. Is it that novelists who do engage in formalistic experimentation, who present in verbal analogues the immediately felt experience through a rich use of images, symbols, and metaphors baffle us?

Looking back over the criticism and the creative writing by Africans in recent years, I think we Africans have been guilty of neglect. We have expended our efforts staking a futile claim on African literature, wasting precious time, attention, and vigour on Western critics to the neglect of African texts. And when we have turned to the literature we have been too eager to demonstrate its – and our own – Africanism to the neglect of the aesthetics of a particular piece. Perhaps it is time we came to the realisation that to be a perceptive critic of African literature demands more than a knowledge of the social realities behind the work or the fortuitous circumstances of one's birth. Literature, like music, requires for successful study a specific faculty, a keen aesthetic sensibility, and a thorough knowledge of the techniques of language.[11]

NOTES

1. Gerald Moore, ed., *African Literature and the Universities* (Ibadan, University Press, 1965), pp. 89–90.
2. 'Language of the Heart', *Présence Africaine*, 30, No. 58, 1966, p. 8.
3. Joseph Okpaku, 'Tradition, Culture, and Criticism', *Présence Africaine*, 70, 1969, p. 141.
4. Ernest Emenyonu, 'African Literature: What Does It Take To Be Its Critic?', *African Literature Today*, 5 (London, Heinemann, 1971), p. 9.
5. Bernth Lindfors, 'Cyprian Ekwensi – An African Popular Novelist', *African Literature Today*, 3 (London, Heinemann, 1969).
6. W. K. Wimsatt, Jr. and Monroe C. Beardsley, *The Verbal Icon* (Kentucky, University of Kentucky Press, 1967).
7. Eustace Palmer, *An Introduction to the African Novel* (London, Heinemann; New York, Africana, 1972), p. xi, comments, '. . . while Ekwensi deserves a feature in any historical discussion of the African novel, it is my opinion that he has no place in a critical work devoted to the masters of African fiction'.

8. Solomon Ogbede Iyasere, *The Rhetoric of African Fiction* (Binghamton, New York, State University of New York, 1972), unpublished dissertation, p. 11.
9. Christopher Heywood, ed., *Perspectives on African Literature*, pp. 117–28, (London, Heinemann; New York, Africana, 1971).
10. Austin J. Shelton, 'Critical Criteria for the Study of African Literature', *Literature East and West*, 12, 1966, p. 10.
11. Tom Creighton, 'Synopsis of Proceedings of Freetown Conference on African Literature', *Transition*, 4, No. 10, 1963, p. 17.

Who does Flora Nwapa write for?

Ernest N. Emenyonu

A recent reviewer of Flora Nwapa's *Idu*[1] concluded by saying: 'Considering her performances in both *Efuru* and *Idu* one cannot help wondering what motivates Miss Nwapa beyond the elementary wish of everyone to be a writer. In her novels there is a complete absence of that phenomenon that has been descibed by various writers as the impulse to write which "kicks you in the pit of your stomach". If this impulse is absent one expects, at least, to be compensated by other things such as beautiful narrative style, amusing and vividly described incidents and powerful characterization. All these are sadly missing in both *Efuru* and *Idu*'.[2]

I have discussed elsewhere,[3] the merits and demerits of Flora Nwapa's *Efuru* (a novel by the way which I have found highly successful in the classroom, highly regarded by most of my students – and undergraduates, black and white alike), so I will try to examine *Idu* in the light of the negative assessment above. One important thing about this criticism of Nwapa's fiction is that it indirectly strikes at some more basic issues in African literary criticism. The question is often asked, 'What is African literature?' Or 'What makes a work of literature African?' The implicit assumption is that African literature is one literary unit for which a single definition can be constructed. Some even ask after reading an African novel 'Is this or that character truly or authentically African?' The concept here again is that there is a single characteristic which identifies one as African. This is no more true than seeking to find a single definition which will serve as an all embracing umbrella for everything that is written as literature in Africa. The African continent is as diverse in tongue as it is in cultural diffusions. This is also true of African literature. It poses for the critic the same type of problem of definition that the term 'African Culture' poses for the sociologist or anthropologist. African literature is not one unit but a totality of all the literary units in Africa – indeed the aggregate of all ethnic and national literatures.

Chinua Achebe speculates that like the rise of individual nation states (after the elimination of white rule in Africa), the next major phase of African literature would be the emergence of group literatures – ethnic and national. In effect, the study of these would provide data that would make generalisations on African literature in general possible.

In another context, Emmanuel Obiechina justifies the need for such ethnic studies as a necessary step to deeper and better understanding and awareness of the nation of which the particular ethnic group is a component part. 'In a multi-ethnic nation like Nigeria, it is imperative that the culture and life-ways of the component units should be given full airing so that national sentiments are built upon the firm foundation of understanding.'[4] This is an essential keynote in the appraisal of works of literature by Africans today.

What is the critic looking for? How does he know when he has found it? The critic has an obligation to his society – he is a kind of guide and teacher to them but it becomes somewhat of an irony when he proves the judge of what more intelligent and sensitive people are reading.

Flora Nwapa's *Idu* like her previous novel, deals with the culture and life-ways of the Igbo and more specifically the fishing and farming residents of Oguta, who find occupation and pleasure in the Oguta Lake, and to whom the 'fantasies' of the 'woman of the lake' are a reality. These are the people about whom Flora Nwapa writes in these novels but this is not enough to make her an authentic Igbo novelist. An Igbo novel (or Igbo literature as a whole) emanates from Igbo life and language. It embraces the social, political, economic, and emotional forms under which Igbo life is manifest. The evaluation of an Igbo work of art is essentially an appreciation of the validity of content as well as the appropriateness of technique. What the writer says about the Igbo is as important as how he says it. Neither alone can constitute his success but the failure in both could mean his failure as an artist. Flora Nwapa's *Idu* is a successful Igbo novel by both standards.

First, what is the novel about? It deals with the theme of barrenness in marriage, something which is of great concern to the Igbo woman because invariably it sets her apart from her friends and associates who are not sure whether her barrenness is as a result of her moral laxity or a divine curse. But if *Idu* is simply about barrenness, how then is it different from the earlier novel *Efuru* and how is it different from John Munonye's *Obi* which deals essentially with the same theme? Idu is a courageous woman, highly successful in her business as a market woman, devoted to her husband but who sadly has no child after several years of marriage. She eventually conceives and has her child on an unusual day – 'the day that we had night in the afternoon. It is a bad day. Pray that the baby does not

29

come today' (p. 84). But the baby Ijoma, did come, bringing with him all the mystery of a child born on the day of an eclipse. But the situation is made more complex because, after her first child, Idu could not conceive again till after four years, and before her delivery her husband dies of a mysterious disease. Idu cannot take it. 'Weep for what?' she asked. 'Weep for Adiewere? That is not what we agreed on. He has cheated me. We did not agree this would happen. We did not agree on what to do if this sort of thing happened. We did not think of it. Why do you want me to weep? I am going with him. Leave me alone. I am going with him' (p. 210). And she actually does. She does not commit suicide nor fall sick at the time and die from it. Rather she eats a nice meal one afternoon, lies down and dies. This is how the author portrays it.

'Anamadi', she called her sister. Anamadi came in. 'Come go and cook for me. I am hungry. I have not eaten for days since Adiewere departed. Go and cook soup with some fish for me.' Anamadi was happy to be useful. Since Adiewere had died she had found it difficult to serve her sister. Idu would not eat anything. She had said things that frightened her. Alone in the room, she had talked to Adiewere as if he was there physically. Some mornings she had greeted him as usual, and laughed when she suddenly remembered that he was no longer there. Anamadi made the fire quickly, sliced the yam and put it over the fire. Then she cut ugu in bits, pounded the pepper and washed the dried fish. Soon the yam was ready. It was ready quickly . . . Idu washed her hands as if she was cleansing them for a ritual. She took a morsel of the food, threw it outside and said it was for Adiewere, the ancestors and the gods, and then she began to eat. . . . Idu ate as she had never eaten before. . . . 'You cooked very well', she told her sister. . . . 'It is well. Sweep the kitchen well. I am going to sleep. I am very tired. When Nwasobi comes, ask her to come inside.' When Nwasobi came, she went into the room. She removed her headtie and fanned herself with it. 'Ewoo, it is warm today, it seems as if it is going to rain.' Idu did not stir. 'Ewoo, Idu this kind of sleep', and as she said this, she went nearer the bed and touched her. Her hand was on Idu's feet when Anamadi came in. 'Is she not up yet? Wake her, she said you should wake her when you come.' Nwasobi did not say a word. Her hand was still on Idu's feet. She did not even look at Anamadi who rushed to Idu's bed saying, 'No, no, it can't be, it's not so. What have I done? Idu, Idu, Idu.' Anamadi called and shook her sister as if by doing so she would bring her back to life. 'Come let's prepare her for the funeral, don't you see she is dead? She kept her word. She has followed her husband. . . .' (pp. 217–18)

Too fantastic? Not if you have been 'listening' to the voices in the novel. Too unrealistic? Not if you have been close enough to the Igbo culture and life-ways. Too remote? Not if you understand that even among the Igbo, the love between two individuals can be such that one can die without the other. Can you recall why in Chinua Achebe's *Things Fall*

Apart it was not possible to beat the drum to tell Umuofia of the death of Ogbuefi Ndulue, the oldest man in Ire? (*Things Fall Apart*, London, 1958, p. 61.) What Flora Nwapa has done is to introduce the reader to a problematic situation in life which takes on an aura of tragedy. In the process she explores in depth the beliefs, aspirations, failures, and successes of the people whose life-ways create the particular human condition in the novel. Tragedy in the Igbo situation is not in the feeling that nothing goes right for the individual, but the fact that any success he attains is followed sooner or later by a bigger and more terrible misfortune. This is a constant reality in Igbo life, which among some Igbo groups is described as the phenomenon of *Ume*. Flora Nwapa writes with a peculiar realism. She brings a feminine closeness and intuition into a theme which has been repeatedly treated by such male Igbo authors as Onuora Nzekwu, John Munonye, Cyprian Ekwensi, among others, but which is best understood in all its ramifications by a woman.

Chinua Achebe once said that no man can understand another whose language he does not speak. But this statement is not as simplistic as it sounds, for Achebe adds 'and "language" here does not mean simply words but a man's entire world-view'.[5] One would have to understand the language of Flora Nwapa's novels in order to appreciate her achievements. This 'language' includes both the Igbo world-view which she communicates and the way she reaches down to all her characters and communicates authentically at all their levels not excluding their idiosyncrasies and mannerisms which she manifests in their speech patterns to help reveal more and more the nature of the characters. There is not one false tone (that is, if you *can* listen carefully) in the voices of these characters whether it is Onyemuru the unmistakable flippant bearer of bad news, or Nwasobi the philosophical antithesis of Onyemuru, or Ishiodu the totally un-diplomatic and nonchalant spendthrift or Adiewere the silently aggressive achiever, or Idu the dignified suffering woman. Flora Nwapa has keen ears for village voices and the know-how to transmit them on the pages of her novel, and what is essentially significant is that she is not necessarily translating Igbo idioms or expressions into English, but in the words of Chinua Achebe she is 'able to expand the English language to suit her Igbo (indeed Oguta) surrounding' and she uses the English language to bring out her message 'without altering it to the extent that its value as a medium of international exchange is lost'.[6]

A few examples will help to illustrate what I mean. When Idu con-templates her fate after the death of her cherished husband, she describes another woman Ojiugo whose life had become meaningless after the death of her former husband (whom she had left because of his impotence but still has deep regard for) in the following manner: 'She "died" the day her husband died. The day Amarajeme died, that was the day she "died" ' (p. 216). Or consider the dialogue between the two small children Ijoma and a playmate as they 'cook for Nwododo' the invisible scapegoat who is 'interesting, and we cheat him all the time. He always loses when we play with him' (p. 116). He is the imaginary figure conceived in the mind of the child, whom the child turns around to beat and defeat when he has suffered similar humiliation. In this regard, a psychological buffer to the child. Again consider Flora Nwapa's way of describing resemblance between father and son. 'As you have seen him, you have seen his father when he was younger. His father vomited him out. But what a pity. I have three other boys, they are all younger than this one and they are all like me. I thank God for that. But the eldest boy will be like his father. Soap cannot wash it off' (p. 122). Consider also Flora Nwapa's handling of the dialogue of the two men, who as they returned from the farm 'fell to talking about the tragedy of Amarajeme who hanged himself from the thatched roof of his hut, with his tongue sticking out "because his wife deserted him". "Come, a man created by God. He searches for a way to die, he does not see one, so he chooses to hang himself. Ewoo, this world is strange." Notice the way in which the conversation acquires a tragic tone as it progresses' (pp. 147–50). These are not exceptions but a consistent thread that weaves through the entire length of the novel.

The realism of her themes and her ever increasing sensitive use of language are two of Flora Nwapa's most enduring qualities as a novelist. Of the former one might tend to say she is over-preoccupied with the concern for children in marriage in an age when the fear of over-population is acute and some ecologists are talking about 'zero population growth', but then among the Igbo (and I fear most Africans) 'what we are all praying for is children. What else do we want if we have children?' (p. 150). One might tend to find Flora Nwapa's characters too talkative and gossipy, and her Ajanupas and Onyemurus too boring by virtue of the same organ that gives them distinction – their tongue – but these novels are mostly about women by a woman, and one should not take lightly the line in which Nwapa says 'You know women's conversation never ends' (p. 97).

The few weaknesses of the novel are minor and depict mainly a failure of proper editorial responsibility. On page 7, there is the wrong tense in 'Idu, it is high time we *see* a dibia'. On page 16, there is the wrong conjunction in '*But* the time Adiewere had finished, Idu had started weeping softly'. On page 18 a name appears twice in a paragraph but is spelled differently – 'Obgenyanu' and 'Ogbenyanu'. On page 82 the wrong noun is used as well as misspelled in 'To the simple folks of the town, it was a great *phenomenan*, unexplained'. On page 90, *not* is used wrongly in place of *nor* in 'She could not eat anything that night, *not* would she tell Adiewere

32

why she was so unhappy'. On page 100, there is this confusing sentence:
'When they touched her (you know our people don't believe in sympath-
ising fully with you unless they have touched you) so they touched her
skin, and it came off from her body.' On page 102, 'glass' is rendered in a
local tone as 'Ganashi' but on page 108, we have 'Ganishi'.

But when everything is considered, *Idu* remains a success in the Igbo
literary tradition. In the appraisal of a work of art by an Igbo, the critic is
looking for a number of things. He should identify the content, the
traditional content in each case. He should show what the author has done
with the traditional material, how he has changed traditional forms to fit
modern conditions. A piece of oral literature (folktale, song, proverb, etc.)
exists as long as it is being performed. The same performance will be
different in the hands of different performers. When it is appreciated, the
critic is really appreciating the art of the performer, rather than the performance itself. At the same time, in appreciating the art of the performer,
the critic would be appreciating quite a lot of things which would be
accepted as criteria for written literature – irony, the shape of the story,
and a certain amount of simple but vivid characterisation. Thus the critic
of African literature has many things to explore beyond 'what motivates'
any particular author to write.

NOTES

1. London, Heinemann, 1970.
2. *Idu*, reviewed by Adeola A. James, *African Literature Today*, No. 5
   (London, Heinemann, 1971), pp. 150–3.
3. *Efuru*, reviewed by Ernest N. Emenyonu, *Ba Shiru*, Journal of the
   Department of African Languages and Literature, University of
   Wisconsin, Madison, Vol. I, No. 1, Spring 1970, pp. 58–61.
4. *The Conch*, Vol. III, No. 2, September 1971, p. 11.
5. 'Where Angels Fear to Tread', *Nigeria Magazine*, No. 75, December
   1962, p. 62.
6. 'The English Language and the African Writer', *Insight*, October/
   December 1966.

Towards a Sociology
of the Nigerian Novel

J. P. O'Flinn

The Nigerian novel has now been with us for twenty years – almost a generation – and it is therefore perhaps the right moment to stand back and try to grasp the roots and meaning of this development.[1]

A good place to start such an undertaking is the standard bibliographies, and a glance at them is revealing. They show that the Nigerian novel first appeared in the 1950s. In that decade there was a slow, even trickle of novels by black African writers, and half of the trickle was Nigerian – eight out of a total of sixteen for the decade. In the 1960s, the trickle became a flow: by 1966, there were thirty-three more novels, and of these almost two-thirds – twenty – had come from Nigeria. But in 1967 the situation changed sharply. In the middle of that year the war between Nigeria and the breakaway state of Biafra started, and it lasted for more than thirty months. In that time novels continued to flow from black African writers at an accelerating rate but the Nigerian novel came almost to a halt: in the three years 1967 to 1969 inclusive the rest of black Africa produced twenty-four novels, Nigeria/Biafra only five, and of these latter the majority were in the hands of the publishers before hostilities started.

The war ended on 15 January 1970, but many felt that the rupture in Nigerian fiction caused by the war would last for some time. Yet statistically, at least, this does not seem to have happened. In 1970 once again, most black African novels were Nigerian. In terms of numbers, it was the best year ever for Nigerian fiction, with new works from Aluko, Amadi, Ike, and Nwapa and first novels from Okpewho and Ulasi, and there is every indication that this generous output will be maintained in the '70s. Or is there?

The developments that lie behind the statistics in the above paragraphs will form the subject of this article, which will attempt to answer perhaps the two most obvious questions that the figures suggest. Firstly, why did

34

the Nigerian novel emerge at the moment that it did – why didn't it appear, say, a generation sooner, or a generation or more later? And secondly, was the civil war simply an unavoidable physical impediment to novel production and will production pick up again as rapidly in the 1970s as the figures already seem to suggest, or has there been a much more fundamental kind of shift which will make the resurgence of the novel in its old form in that part of West Africa more or less impossible?

In order to arrive at outlines of answers to these questions in the course of a single article, certain things will have to be taken for granted if any new ground is to be broken at all. I shall, for example, assume that the existence of connections between, on the one hand, the novel form and its rise in a given society and, on the other, a bourgeoisie and its self-articulation, is a fact familiar to readers. This has been fully argued by critics as diverse as Georg Lukács and Ian Watt and needs no further rehearsal here. Once the existence of the connections is allowed, then the way is clear for an analysis of the particular forms they took in the Nigerian situation, and it is in the examination of these forms that answers to the questions set out above will begin to emerge.

I

For novels to be written at all, there are two obvious prerequisites: the novelist must have something to say and there must be a sizeable group of people who want to hear it. Obvious though this may be, it at once sets the novel apart from various branches of the fine arts which can flourish as long as there is a relatively small elite with sufficient surplus income to subsidise their operations. They therefore do not require the much larger following that the novel, because of the different economic structures inherent in its production and distribution, demands if it is to appear and survive at all. To put it another way: if the artist knows there is a potential buyer for his painting, he can go ahead and paint; but the novelist has to be assured of the existence of several thousand potential buyers before he can function as a novelist. Before buyers can be present in these numbers, the society in which the novelist works must have reached a certain stage of development. There must, for example, be a sizeable percentage of the population that is both literate and that has an income sufficiently high to make the purchase of books feasible after the bare necessities of life have been catered for.

It is at this point that it has been objected that Nigerian society has not reached such a stage, or, even if it has, that its novelists are not really catering for it but are using the outlets provided by international publishers to address a cosmopolitan and largely non-African, let alone non-Nigerian audience. There is no point in denying that, granted market structures, some Nigerian fiction inevitably is of this type: an unobjectionable example, here would be Onuora Nzekwu's *Wand of Noble Wood* with its several set-piece passages clearly aimed at enlightening overseas readers. Yet equally it needs to be insisted that this kind of thing is not the rule. Achebe, to take another case, would argue that he writes for Lagos rather than London and in his famous statement 'The Novelist as Teacher'[2] he provides figures to support his claim. Paperback sales of *Things Fall Apart* in 1963 were 20,000 in Nigeria, 800 in the United Kingdom, and 2,500 in the rest of the world, and those of *No Longer at Ease* followed the same pattern. However this huge proportion (over 85 per cent) of sales within Nigeria was achieved – and plainly much of it would derive, for example, from compulsory prescription in schools – as far as Achebe and his intentions are concerned, it means that his audience is primarily composed of fellow countrymen and his writing is shaped accordingly.

How did this audience arise and how did novelists appear to cater for them? What are the significant particularities of the national history that help to determine the aspirations and perspectives of both authors and readers? To answer these questions an examination of the roots of present-day Nigeria is necessary, and since both novel form and the language that Nigerian novelists tend to use are European in origin, it would seem sensible to start such an examination at the point where forces from Europe assumed decisive control of Nigerian society. This point is the colonisation of Nigeria at the end of the nineteenth century. Lagos was the first area to be annexed, in 1861, and by 1914 the whole of modern Nigeria had been expropriated.

In the following years changes were initiated in the economic and social structure of the country by the colonial power to facilitate that exploitation of manpower and natural resources which had been the major motive for annexation. Most important of these for present purposes was the building of a network of communications essential if the produce of the hinterland was to pass through the southern ports to the outside world. Between 1895 and 1940, 2,203 miles of rail were laid across the Federation, and in recent years (despite some closures) additions to this network have been made in the Northern region. Road building came later, but when it came it was equally spectacular: although as late as 1937 there was only one tarred road outside the towns, by 1969 the country was covered by 55,000 miles of road, nearly 20 per cent of them tarred.

The growth of this network was closely linked to economic needs. As Arthur Norton Cook, for example, puts it: 'When the discovery of a port on Bonny Creek, later named Port Harcourt, was followed by the discovery of coal at Udi, all objections to a railroad in this [Eastern] region vanished.'[3] At once we find the basis laid for the growth of a town at Port Harcourt: it becomes a natural point for capital investment and hence in turn draws in under-employed masses from surrounding agricultural areas. Thus, in 1921 the population of Port Harcourt was 7,000; by 1953 it had grown to 72,000; and by the start of the civil war it was 180,000. There were similar developments all over the Federation – at close on three-quarters of a million in 1963 the population of Lagos, for example, had doubled in ten years. In 1969 it was estimated that there were a dozen Nigerian cities with populations of over 100,000, while 'about 20 per cent of the population live in towns of more than 20,000 inhabitants and this percentage is growing steadily'.[4]

Ian Watt regards eighteenth-century urbanisation, and especially the phenomenal growth of London, as central to the rise of the English novel.[5] London, with its large literate audience and with half the book-sellers of England, provided for the first time the conditions wherein a functioning novel form was feasible. Twentieth-century Nigeria has a series of cities whose size is not matched anywhere in black Africa, and it is therefore possible to see Nigeria's domination of the first decades of the African novel as explicable in part by its high degree of urbanisation and the favourable conditions this provides. Walter Schwarz, on a visit to Ibadan (whose population of 1.3 million makes it the largest African city south of the Sahara), was particularly struck by the 'thousands of tiny shops and ramshackle factories (there must be a thousand bookshops and several hundred small printing works)'.[6] Bookshops do not of themselves, of course, produce novels, nor indeed do they multiply unless a market already exists, but nonetheless their presence in such numbers in major urban centres did provide an array of local outlets for aspiring Nigerian novelists that was not available to the same extent to their potential counterparts in, say, Ghana or Kenya. As we have already seen, paperback sales of *Things Fall Apart* in Nigeria in 1963 were 20,000: it is difficult to imagine any other country in black Africa having the kind of distribution network to make it able to match novel sales of that order.

II

If, as was suggested earlier, the first appearance of the novel in a given society is dependent upon the emergence of a bourgeoisie, it becomes important for present purposes to establish the point in Nigerian history when such a class began to shape itself and articulate its needs. Ken Post sees the mushroom growth of West African towns as creating within the

37

urban masses elements of a 'bourgeoisie' in the literal sense which provided the leadership for the independence movements.[7] Between the two world wars, however, these elements were too small to threaten the colonial power, and when, through the National Congress of British West Africa, they began in 1920 to request a greater degree of local autonomy, they were treated peremptorily by the Colonial Secretary, Lord Milner, and furiously denounced by Sir Hugh Clifford, the Governor of Nigeria. Their successors were greeted with similar contempt in 1943: Nnamdi Azikiwe, the future President of Nigeria, led a group of Nigerian journalists visiting London and submitted a memorandum to the British Government entitled 'The Atlantic Charter and British West Africa', calling *inter alia* for eventual independence. The Colonial Office ignored the memorandum.

And yet within a very few years Azikiwe was one of the leaders of a nationalist movement which the British Government accepted as the source of future rulers. This change can be traced to a variety of causes. The Second World War itself certainly accounts for it in part. As the Smythes note in their study of the rise of the new Nigerian elite 'the necessity (created by war requirements) for withdrawing colonial personnel for duty elsewhere accelerated the process of enlarging the powers of the three territories and reducing the functions of the government administration at Lagos'.[8] Not only did the elite begin to find itself for the first time closer to positions of something like power, but it also found that the war had helped to create for it the beginnings of a genuinely popular following that it had lacked when, a generation earlier, Governor Clifford had been able to dismiss it as unrepresentative and Europeanised. (The fact that the good Governor himself was both of these did not, we may presume, disqualify him, at least in his own eyes.)

Two important products of the war helped to create this popular following. In the first place the Colonial Development and Welfare Act of 1940 stipulated the formation of unions and hence their number rose in Nigeria from a dozen with 500 members at the start of the war to 85 with 30,000 members at its close. Secondly, as membership rose, the union movement was at the same time given an issue on which to fight: as part of its war-time measures, the colonial administration tightened its control over the economy and this showed itself most notably in an attempt to freeze incomes at a time when inflationary pressures set up by the war were effectively cutting incomes. The result was a general strike in 1945, the first in Nigerian history, that lasted for thirty-seven days and involved seventeen major unions, and the discontent that this indicates also expressed itself in the creation of a series of political parties to articulate and direct increasing unrest. Azikiwe had founded the National Council for Nigeria and the Cameroons in 1944, the Action Group emerged not

38

long afterwards, and the Northern People's Congress appeared in 1949, which year also witnessed another series of strikes. The tone of the leadership took on a new militancy to reflect the growing struggle – the Fifth Pan-African Congress, for example, held at Manchester in 1945 was the first of such congresses to make outright demands for independence.

If we are to understand the forces that shaped and determined the make-up and the ideology of the Nigerian elite that eventually came to power in 1960, it is essential to grasp from the start the attitude of the colonial government towards that elite. Firm opposition would have delayed the process of transition to independence, would have led to the replacement of moderate elements within the elite by a more militant leadership, and could eventually have precipitated a war of Algerian proportions. But no such war was to come until after independence, until after the elite began to fall apart. Instead, in the 1940s and 1950s, the British administration conducted a fairly orderly retreat, oepning most doors when nationalists began to lean on them at all heavily.

Why? Imperialism had not become benevolent, and the experience of Malaya and Northern Ireland were to show that it was capable of waging a bitter fight where it sensed a genuine threat to its deepest interests. What had occurred was a shift in the structure of capitalism, and just as earlier shifts had precipitated first the slave trade, then its suppression, and finally the annexation of the colony, so too this latest restructuring prompted something akin to acceptance of the drive towards 'independence' in most parts of the British Empire. Briefly, the shift was as follows: before the First World War, 90 per cent of British overseas investment was held in 'portfolios' of shares in loans to colonial and other governments. After the Second World War, the pattern was very different: most of the capital outflow took the form of direct investment in branches and subsidiaries of home companies. Plainly, political control of the colonial state was now less vital than in the days when the colonial government itself had been the major investment. More crucial now was the need of British capital to ally itself, in the face of American, German, and French competition, with the indigenous bourgeoisie in order to ensure favourable terms for expansion in the indigenous market which was now the major source of profit. Thus it need come as no surprise that in the late '50s and early '60s it was a Conservative British Government that handed out flags and constitutions to streams of African leaders. In 1957 there were only ten independent states in Africa; by 1963 there were thirty-four.

Granted, therefore, that the British ruling class had implicitly conceded the independence struggle in its early stages, various policies adopted in Nigeria are at once comprehensible. A capitalist (as opposed to pre-capitalist) economy functioning in the second half of the twentieth century

39

requires a high degree of literacy and training amongst both working and bureaucratic classes, and hence no substantial barriers were placed in the way of nationalist demands for a rapid expansion of the education programme. Less than 2 per cent of primary-school-age children in Nigeria were attending school in 1934; by 1958, the figure was 36 per cent and still growing. Between 1962 and 1965, the government of the Western Region, the first in black Africa to introduce free primary schooling, was spending 40 per cent of its budget on education, as was the Eastern Region, and the national target, set in 1960, of 10,000 university students by 1970 was reached in 1966. In 1949 only 5 per cent of the population were literate, yet within little more than a decade the basis for the elimination of illiteracy was laid. In 1949, therefore, a novel in any sense speaking to the Nigerian people was plainly impossible. Yet by the middle '50s it at least became worth the effort, and by the early '60s, as we have seen, sales figures indicate that the audience had come into being.

III

Use has been made several times so far of terms such as elite, bourgeoisie and so on, and connections suggested between them and the Nigerian novelists, and it is necessary before going any further to define these terms more precisely. During the period under consideration, a genuine class of capitalists scarcely existed in Nigeria: Schwarz guessed in 1968 that there were perhaps only twenty 'tycoons' in the whole country. Smythe and Smythe estimate that the whole elite on independence eve consisted of some 20,000 persons, and amongst these very few were major businessmen. Most were government officials, educators, lawyers, and traditional rulers. Only 12 per cent were businessmen, simply because most business was in British, Syrio-Lebanese, Greek, French, Indian, and American hands. This was to have grave consequences after independence, as will be seen later. For the rest, estimates of those engaged in subsistence pursuits on the land vary, but a guess of 75 per cent of the adult population seems plausible. T. M. Yesufu conjectured in 1962 that there were 800,000 industrial wage earners, approximately 2 per cent of the whole population, while Adebayo Adedeji has found that 99 per cent of Nigerian tax-payers are within the annual income range of £50 to £700.[9]

What emerges, then, is a complex picture: the primitive communism of the villages has been in decay since at least the tenth century, when the introduction of slavery and the setting up of various West African states marked a new stage of evolution. On the other hand, despite the oil rigs in the Niger Delta, the tin mines of the Jos Plateau and the coalfield at

40

Enugu, full-scale capitalist development in the past had been retarded by the largely foreign ownership of the means of production, distribution, and exchange, and also by the artificial preservation in Northern Nigeria of feudal forms and hierarchies in order to facilitate indirect rule during the colonial period. In short, while class structures clearly exist, Nigerian society presents a confused picture of intersecting and coexisting forms as the growth of new class distinctions flowing from the imposition of a capitalist economy takes place in a context of variously decaying pre-capitalist formations. In its current stage of nervous and rapid transition, that society has less of the clearly defined and historically grounded class distinctions, less of the deep-rooted and flourishing cultural, political and social institutions which grow out of those distinctions, than other societies at other, more stable moments.

These facts had a direct bearing on the politics of the pre-independence era. The low level of industrialisation meant that the proletariat alone was too small to organise and conduct the battle for independence. The foreign penetration of the business community likewise meant that alone the bourgeoisie was not able to muster enough power to drive the British out. Only by acting together could they mount the kind of potential threat which the British administration, aware of the real interests of the metropolitan ruling class, would not attempt to contest in any serious fashion. Moreover, such an alliance was possible because both classes shared a common interest – namely the removal of the overt British presence as a necessary prelude to the fuller development of both – and both were sufficiently recent historical phenomena to obviate the possibility of a deep-rooted class-consciousness growing out of and feeding back into class struggles which might make alliance difficult.

Thus it was that the urban proletariat, the crowds of under-employed and unemployed in the shanty towns, and the rural masses fell willingly into line behind the demands for national independence voiced by the local wealthy and the bourgeoisie through the political parties. These parties by and large represented the interests of a developing bourgeois class: in a country where businessmen formed only a tiny fraction of the population, they nonetheless constituted over 37 per cent of the A.G. leadership at a local level in the Western Region in 1958. (In addition, over 24 per cent were educators of various kinds and over 21 per cent were members of other professions. N.C.N.C. percentages were very similar. In the same year, 27 per cent of the members of the N.P.C. National Executive Committee were businessmen and 24 per cent educators.) The parties' twin demands of the '40s and '50s for independence and Nigerianisation were ones that could be taken up by all classes. It was not until after 1960, that the alliances formed behind these slogans began to crumble when it became a question of independence for whom and promotion for which Nigerians. Then it became clear that what the slogans had been designed to produce were not structural changes but rather changes in the personnel manning those structures. The antagonisms and contradictions generated by those structures would plainly, after an initial period of euphoria, remain the same and once more reassert themselves.

But in the years immediately after the Second World War these problems lay far in the future, and it was possible then for the N.C.N.C. with its overwhelmingly bourgeois membership to have eighty trade unions affiliated to it before it was twelve months old. Struggles waged by workers fed directly into the nationalist struggle led by the politicians. Thus, for example, in 1949 a British officer panicked and ordered troops to fire on a crowd of striking miners in Enugu: twenty-one were killed and fifty-one wounded, and there was at once a series of nationalist uprisings throughout the Eastern Region. The British, in their various roles as employers, administrators, army officers and so on, came invariably into conflict with local interests on a whole series of levels and it was natural that, at any point where conflict flared, other local interests would take the side of their compatriots against a common enemy.

As the nation moved towards independence this alliance began to subside: the advent of a Nigerian as Minister of Labour in 1951, for example, at once blurred what had seemed to be a clear community of interest between bourgeoisie and proletariat, and the 1964 General Strike, with unions pitted against an indigenous government, was a very different affair from the one in 1945, when N.C.N.C. speakers toured the nation and raised £13,500 for the strikers. In 1969 the Federal Military Government made it an offence to threaten, organise, encourage or even to do an act preparatory to organising a strike. The days of collections for strikers, of heady rhetoric by businessmen-politicians about 'pragmatic socialism', have now given way to gaol for trade unionists, and soldier-politicians with little interest in flattering the aspirations of wage earners.

IV

Briefly, that is what happened in Nigeria in the years leading up to independence. Where does the novel fit into this process? If we turn back to the figures given at the beginning of the article, we see that the Nigerian novel bestrides the year of Nigerian independence, 1960: it struggles to its feet in the half-decade before independence and then reaches a peak in the half-decade after it. The novel then declines at the same time as the various alliances formed to secure independence begin to fly violently

42

apart. Then in 1970 conflict subsides and the novel re-emerges. It remains to be seen whether this parallel movement is coincidental or evidence of a deep causal relationship.

Certainly, colonial rule has usually acted as a deterrent to healthy literary production: from the experience of the early-nineteenth-century Cuban slave Juan Francisco Manzano, tortured by his owner for writing poems, to the mass round-ups by the French of Algerian story-tellers during the Algerian War, imperialists have always been clear about the potentially subversive nature of literature, and, where they have not actively suppressed it, have by their very presence and domination inhibited the growth of that indigenous leisure class without which neither the production nor the enjoyment of art is possible on any sizeable scale.

As we have seen already, the changing nature of capitalism dictated a British withdrawal from direct imperial control in the years after the Second World War. Into the vacuum induced by this movement were sucked an indigenous elite fostered by a rapidly expanding education system. This fostering is clear in other spheres as well as in education. In the 1950s David Williams, the English managing director of the *West African Review*, *Daily Times* (published in Nigeria), *Daily Graphic* (Gold Coast – later Ghana) and *Daily Mail* (Sierra Leone) provided encouragement and outlets for budding fiction writers in the pages of his journals, as did the British editor of *Drum*, a magazine published in South Africa. Davidson Nicol estimated in 1956 that, of avenues of expression open to West African writers, 'by far the most important has been the British Broadcasting Corporation. It has a special weekly programme called "West African Voices" devoted to original writing by West Africans'.[10] The British Council, 'that unique and helpful patron of the arts' in Nicol's view, organised a whole series of literary competitions to promote Nigerian writing. Then, in 1962, the London publishers Heinemann launched their African Writers Series, which aimed to make a range of African writing, principally novels, readily available in cheap paperback form. From the start, they were the publishers, with only one or two exceptions, of the major Nigerian novelists, and were clearly an essential prerequisite for the surge forward which Nigerian fiction made in the years immediately following.

Of course, the fact that Nigerian literature was, in its first decades, almost entirely in the hands of European impresarios generated a variety of problems and distortions, some of which were referred to earlier. The explosion in African education after 1945 meant that for the first time profits were to be made in catering for the reading requirements of the continent, and it was European capital that took advantage of the situation.

43

Robert P. Armstrong, in a 1966 survey of Nigerian book publishing, conceded the semi-literate market to the indigenous press, but concluded: 'Publishing for literates, however, is not yet in any significant sense indigenous, since it has depended on European capital and talent to cater to essentially European-derived needs.'[11] Thus even Mbari Publications of Ibadan, often held up as an example of Nigerian publishing and the first to produce the works of John Pepper Clark and Wole Soyinka, was in fact founded by a German, Ulli Beier, and supported by the Congress for Cultural Freedom, a creature of the C.I.A.

However, the point being made here is that, for historical reasons that have already been outlined, Western capital and Western institutions provided Nigerian authors with facilities – which were neither previously available, nor available indigenously – to have their work published on an unprecedented scale. From the start, Nigerian novelists were given access by their international backers to an international market, and thus novel production was possible on a scale which would not have been feasible had they been limited to the small, albeit growing, home market. Thus, by contrast, in Nkrumah's Ghana, where entirely justifiable attempts were made to set up a state publishing house and state book distribution to ease the strain exerted by the book trade on the nation's financial resources, the novel, in effect confined to the tiny home market, was not a flourishing form.

The first dozen Nigerian novelists who came forward to cater for the market thus supplied form a remarkably homogeneous group. They were: Timothy Aluko (b. 1918); Amos Tutuola (b. 1920); Cyprian Ekwensi (b. 1921); Gabriel Okara (b. 1921); Onuora Nzekwu (b. 1928); John Munonye (b. 1929); Chinua Achebe (b. 1930); Vincent Ike (b. 1931); Flora Nwapa (b. 1931); Elechi Amadi (b. 1934); Wole Soyinka (b. 1934); and Nkem Nwankwo (b. 1936). With only three exceptions (Aluko, Soyinka and Tutuola), they were all Easterners and, with the exception again of Tutuola, all could be fairly described as belonging to the upper levels of the bourgeoisie. Eight of them (Aluko, Ekwensi, Okara, Achebe, Ike, Amadi, Soyinka and Nwankwo) went to one of the four or five government colleges and seven (Munonye, Achebe, Ike, Nwapa, Amadi, Soyinka and Nwankwo) were at University College, Ibadan, the first Nigerian university. Drawn as they were from a tiny elite, their links with the governing class were naturally strong, and at least two-thirds of them have at some time or other worked in branches of the government or civil service.

In short, they are fairly clearly identifiable as a group within the nascent Nigerian bourgeoisie during the years when that class secured positions of national power. Their works, in the terms suggested by Lucien Goldmann, both spring from the world-view of an identifiable social group and act

44

back on that world-view, constantly modifying and extending it. It is within this process of extension and modification that, to take one example, Achebe's novels in the main locate themselves, whereas the works of a more clearly conservative man like Aluko reflect bourgeois values in a fairly direct way. Ekwensi in his novels about Lagos life is almost unaware of the existence of the crowds in the shanty towns. Heroes tend to be journalists (Ekwensi's *People of the City*; Nzekwu's *Wand of Noble Wood*) or university graduates (Achebe's *No Longer at Ease*; Ike's *Toads for Supper*), heroines comparatively wealthy and independent figures (Ekwensi's *Jagua Nana*; Amadi's *The Concubine*).

However, this perspective creates no problems for the writer as long as the bourgeoisie remain a progressive class, and this the Nigerian bourgeoisie undoubtedly was during the years when it led the independence movement. Thus the novelist was able to reflect and extend the consciousness of a class, his own class, whose interests seemed to coincide with those of the nation as a whole. As the bourgeoisie began to assert and articulate itself after seventy years of dependent status, so too did the nation, and so too did the novelists in their sphere. For a decade, the Nigerian novel was carried forward on a wave of popular forces, all bearing in the same direction and at last seemingly unimpeded. When, independence achieved, this wave crashed to the ground, reformed into its mutually antagonistic parts and was confronted again wtih external impediments, then the novel too briefly subsided.

V

We noted earlier that, although expatriate ownership of the major means of production and distribution prevented full-scale capitalist development and the concomitant full-scale growth of classes, nonetheless the needs of the colonial economy generated a range of trades and professions which represented the beginnings of class differentiation. As the British administration withdrew, a ruling elite was drawn from amongst these classes and was the subject of an eve-of-independence study, *The New Nigerian Elite*, by Hugh H. and Mabel M. Smythe.

The book uses the terms 'elite' and 'ruling class' interchangeably; it is ownership of the means of production which is normally regarded as constituting the basis of a ruling class. Yet on page 85 we find this:

Although there are some Nigerians in small manufacturing or other enterprises, no Nigerian individual or group as yet controls any large industrial development, such as mining, railways, or general manufacturing, or such industries as petroleum, beverages, tobacco growing and manufacturing, cement making, department store retailing, textile milling, shipping, or the export-import business.

Included here is almost every area of Nigerian life capable of large-scale capital generation. Some examples: Nigerian oil production is the fastest growing in the world, and estimates suggest that in 1973 it will reach two million barrels a day. Nigeria provides three-quarters of the world's annual supply of columbium and is the world's largest supplier of palm-oil products. (Here a virtual monopoly is exercised by the United Africa Company, a Unilever subsidiary.) Statistics on the extent of foreign penetration of the conomy are unreliable, but the results of the penetration are clear enough. Siphoning off by overseas interests of profits means a poor rate of indigenous capital formation, and the problem is compounded by predominantly foreign ownership and operation of the banking system.

These facts placed the political elite who came to power in 1960 in an untenable position. They discovered that that acceleration out of 'under-development' which was the major popular aspiration now that independence was achieved was impossible without either the possession of colonies, crucial to the development of the Western world, or full control over the profits generated by Nigerian labour.

There are, of course, revolutionary ways of breaking out of this bind, but these the elite were not prepared to take, and this makes British readiness to withdraw from direct control, discussed earlier, easier to understand. Dr Nnamdi Azikiwe, first President of Nigeria and owner of a string of West African newspapers, has been called Nigeria's Lord Thomson, and is not a revolutionary for the same obvious reasons that his lordship is not. The dire clichés that poured from his pen at the time of independence ('favourable climate for capital investment ... *Pax Britannica* ... the right of the people of Nigeria to live in a society which respects free enterprise ... the Commonwealth is an institution which buttresses the crusade for peace and international co-operation')[12] were enough to reassure overseas investors that there would be no nonsense about nationalisation or socialism from the new leaders of Nigeria. That being the case, that leadership had perforce to disregard their own populist rhetoric of the last decades and content themselves with feathering their own nests, only venturing outside to take strong measures against their disillusioned followers (now called 'subversives'.)[13]

The contradiction here between the desire of the elite to secure their own position and widespread hopes, generated by the independence movement, of an improvement in the quality of life for the people as a whole, and the attempt to resolve this contradiction within the intolerably narrow limits imposed by a developing economy whose control, as we have seen, did not

46

rest in Nigerian hands, led in combination to a series of crises running through the general strike of 1964 and the bitterly disputed Federal and Western elections of 1965 to the two coups of 1966 and the civil war which began in 1967.

Paradoxically, these years of accelerating breakdown were also the most productive years in the brief history of the Nigerian novel. At the very time that the intricate network of national and class alliances, which created the conditions and the consciousness that made the Nigerian novel possible, was rapidly disintegrating, that novel enjoyed its most fruitful period. Yet this is only an apparent paradox, and it is not really surprising to find writers working out of a consciousness whose basis has begun to disappear. Thus, at the point of breakdown, we find some novelists still dealing in the illusions of their class but at the same time we find the best of them aware of the shifting ground beneath their feet and fighting to extend the consciousness of their readers to meet the realities emerging through the massive changes of the 1960s.

The result was what Arthur Ravenscroft has called the novels of dis-illusion:[14] Gabriel Okara's *The Voice* (1964), Wole Soyinka's *The Inter-preters* (1965), and Chinua Achebe's *A Man of the People* (1966), novels aware, in varying degrees, of the contradictions in mid-sixties Nigeria, conscious of the way they are ripening towards social breakdown, and striving to meet and somehow intervene in this situation. The problem posed by *The Voice*, for example, is the difficulty of opposition in an already corrupt but highly chauvinist (because newly independent) state, a state suspicious of intellectuals like the hero Okolo (although the leaders who like stirring up populist anti-intellectualism are themselves graduates), a state which tries to blackmail its people into averting their eyes from scandals.

Okara is aware here of the size of the crisis in ways that, for example, those members of the political elite shortly to be assassinated or imprisoned were not, and in this sense his novel represents a real extension of the consciousness of his social group. And yet in other ways he is unable to pass beyond the limits of that group-consciousness and hence is as unable as the political elite he rightly attacks to find solutions to the problem he has posed. Thus, he regards the people as an undifferentiated and ignorant mass, 'the knowing-nothing footsteps, the bad footsteps', scarcely human at all – sometimes, as the text suggests, more like a pack of dogs or a colony of ants. This disdain for the people means that they are seen, along with the political elite, as part of the problem rather than its potential solution, and, granted this perspective, the novel is forced to pose a different kind of elitism as the only hope for the future.

Soyinka is a more cosmopolitan figure than any of his Nigerian colleagues and hence his work has dimensions that do not originate locally and that therefore take it outside the scope of this article. Nonetheless, an especially instructive comparison could be made, for example, between the funeral of the fictional nationalist hero De Pereira, described with almost naive piety in 1954 by Cyprian Ekwensi in *People of the City*, and the bitter mockery with which *The Interpreters* surrounds the funeral of a similar figure, Sir Derinola. The gap between the two accounts, even allowing for personal differences between the two authors, is the measure of a vast shift of consciousness in little more than a decade.

The break between the literary and the political elite had been sharply signalled by Soyinka's first imprisonment – the charge was sabotaging a broadcast by the Western Region Premier – before Achebe's *A Man of the People* was published at the beginning of 1966 to provide further evidence of the split. Achebe's novel rejects both the old political elite and the new intellectual pseudo-radical elite, in whom Okara placed some hope, to arrive at an instinctive, tentative confidence in the 'will of the whole people', though the novel breaks off when confronted with the problem of transferring this will from the local level, where it functions well, to the wider, confused national scene. It is here that Achebe moves beyond the spit in the eye of the nearest establishment figure with which Soyinka closes *The Interpreters* – a gesture of defiance, but scarcely of change. It is this positive growth of consciousness that makes *A Man of the People*, for all its occasional stridencies and lack of polish, Achebe's most interesting achievement.

VI

The cabinet of the Federal Government was decimated during Major Nzeogwu's abortive coup in January 1966 and its rump handed over power to Major General Ironsi. It did so to the accompaniment of widespread rejoicing which indicated the extent of popular disillusion with the old regime and above all with its corruption.

The question of corruption is one that needs to be handled with care because commentators so often present it in racialist terms, with implicit suggestions that Sambo is only two generations down from the trees and hence cannot be expected to have the highly developed ethical sense of British politicians and businessmen. The fact of course is that if one uses sources of information other than, say, the editorial columns of the *Daily Telegraph* the ethics of the British (or indeed of any) ruling class do not stand up to real inspection. But analysis and response need to go deeper than this. The problem is that whereas in the so-called Free World it is

48

regarded as right for a group to expropriate the labour of the people and divert it towards private goals, it is at the same time paradoxically regarded as wrong for a group to expropriate the taxes of the people and divert them towards private goals. This paradox was particularly pressing in Nigeria where, as we have seen, ownership of the means of production and the banks was largely in non-Nigerian hands and hence the capital accumulated by government and by government agencies and marketing boards remained almost the only source really open to the indigenous entrepreneur. He therefore found himself confined to swindling frantically within the narrow margins that independence conceded. The result was a conspicuous misdirection of public funds and the enrichment of a few at the expense of the many on whose continued support the few depended – an explosive situation, as events in 1966 and beyond indicated.

Yet the officers who were handed power in January 1966 were in no sense revolutionaries. The problems therefore remained the same, the contradictions were still as sharp, and hence the new leader, Major General Ironsi, shortly met the same fate, namely assassination, as his predecessor. Further disintegration marked the following months and culminated in the civil war that lasted from May 1967 to January 1970. In less than a decade those national alliances across class and region which had presented a reasonably united front in the pursuit of independence lay in ruins.

The breakdown involved Nigerian writers in ways that would obviously preclude literary activity. Amadi and Soyinka suffered spells of imprisonment. The poet Christopher Okigbo was killed. Ekwensi, Okara and Achebe all worked for the breakaway Biafran Government. Aluko (Director of Public Works, Western State), Nwapa (Commissioner for Health and Social Welfare, East Central State) and Amadi (acting Permanent Secretary, Ministry of Information) were in their different offices heavily caught up in reconstruction work in the post-war period.

Yet if we examine the case of Achebe in a little detail we see that it is something more than a mere inability to find time to write or be heard above the chatter of bullets and thud of bombs. In 1969, in the course of a pro-Biafran speaking tour of the United States, he gave an interview which began with a Fanonist critique of certain kinds of African literature:

. . . the culture of a people is more than books and poems. It is their cooperative effort to make a clearing in the jungle and build on it a place of human habitation. . . . So while the African intellectual was busily displaying the past culture of Africa, the troubled peoples of Africa were already creating new revolutionary cultures which took into account their present conditions. As long as people are alive, their culture is alive; as long as people are changing, their culture will be changing. The only place where culture is static, and exists independently of

people, is the museum, and this is not an African institution. . . . .
This has been the problem of the African artist: he has been left far behind by the people who make culture, and he must now hurry and catch up with them – to borrow the beautiful expression of Fanon – in that zone of occult instability where the people dwell.[15]

Having thus ruled out more novels of the type to which *Things Fall Apart* and *Arrow of God* belong, Achebe went on to rule out novel writing altogether for the moment:

> I can create, but of course not the kind of thing I created when I was at ease. I can't write a novel now. I wouldn't want to. And even if I wanted to, I couldn't. So that particular artistic form is out for me at the moment. I can write poetry – something short, intense, more in keeping with my mood. I can write essays. I can even lecture. All this is creating in the context of our struggle. At home I do a lot of writing, but not fiction, something more concrete, more directly related to what's going on. What I'm saying is that there are forms of creativity which suit different moments. I wouldn't consider writing a poem on daffodils particularly creative in my situation now. It would be foolish; I couldn't do it. But there are plays – about the Biafran war. I've seen two really excellent plays and an opera, the title of which is the name of one of the weapons that Biafran scientists developed. (pp. 17–18)

As the figures given at the beginning of the article would indicate, Achebe was not alone in reacting to the war in this way.

But the conditions which generated a statement of this kind, conditions captured briefly in the opening of Achebe's short story *Girls at War*, have disappeared and Nigeria now faces the future under the rule of a military government described by Roger Murray several years ago as repressive, financially conservative, and culturally null.[16] In this context it is illuminating if depressing to contrast the bold horizons that Achebe glimpsed during the war with the task (which by comparison seems prim and arty) that he is now involved in: ·

> I am trying through a new literary magazine *Okike* to discover new writers, publish them, and to create proper critical standards.[17]

Statements of this kind can only derive from an elite large and stable enough to be able to afford the luxury of such an undertaking. There is evidence that suggests that the provision of that stability is a major aim of the Federal Military Government. Certainly it is making vigorous efforts to widen the perilously narrow economic base of the indigenous bourgeoisie which narrowness, as we have seen, did much to bring the post-independence federation tumbling down. Indigenisation decrees, for example, have reserved twenty-two areas of enterprise exclusively for Nigerians and banned a further thirty-three to aliens under certain conditions. Oil, the crucial commodity, is unsurprisingly not on this list but those businesses that are will open up sectors of the economy from which the small Nigerian entrepreneur was in the past wholly or partly excluded. This, in combination with accelerating oil revenues, post-war reconstruction and the stimulus provided by the shift to metrification and decimalisation, should provide boom conditions in Nigeria for the immediate future, and this is already being reflected in the surge forward in the index of industrial production and in the strength of the Nigerian currency.

It was argued at the start of the article that the Nigerian novel rose at the same time as the national bourgeoisie moved into positions of political power. Because that class was at that time too small to support a flourishing novel by itself and because for a brief period the class expressed the aspirations of a whole nation, the Nigerian novel at its best grew out of a particular kind of consciousness (resulting from these conditions) that constituted much of its quality. To put it negatively, it avoided, because of its social situation, the inbred texture of literature which, in Orwell's phrase, appears to be written solely by literary gents for literary gents about literary gents and which abounds in other, differently structured societies.

The various alliances out of which statements of that kind could grow collapsed when the ruling elite proved incapable of realising the aspirations of independence. Alliance gave way to traumatic conflict. It is still too early to trace clearly the outlines of post-war structures but if, as has been already suggested, a major feature of them will be an expanded and more economically stable bourgeoisie, we may expect the Nigerian novel, like other novels, to locate itself increasingly within that class and its aspirations, contradictions, and preoccupations. Essentially national novels like *People of the City* and *Things Fall Apart* would in such a context more and more give way to a more privatised, alienated fiction, work at once increasingly sophisticated and increasingly limited. It is in this sense that perhaps *The Interpreters* will one day be seen as a forerunner of the second generation of Nigerian novels.

NOTES

1. In order to do as much as outline the kind of model the title promises, it has been necessary for me to suppress as far as possible discussion of particular works. Any full treatment of the subject would of course require the illustration and support that such discussion alone can

provide, and I hope to be able to publish such a treatment elsewhere before too long.

2. *New Statesman*, 29 January 1965.
3. *British Enterprise in Nigeria* (London, 1943), p. 221.
4. International Trade Centre (UNCTAD/GATT), *Nigeria: The Market for Selected Engineering Products from Developing Countries* (Geneva, 1969), p. 4.
5. *The Rise of the Novel* (London, Chatto and Windus, 1957), pp. 184–7.
6. *Nigeria* (London, 1968), p. 9.
7. *The New States of West Africa* (London, Penguin, 1968), p. 50.
8. Hugh H. and Mabel M. Smythe, *The New Nigerian Elite* (Stanford, 1960), p. 22.
9. See *An Introduction to Industrial Relations in Nigeria* (London, O.U.P., 1962), p. 14, and *Nigerian Federal Finance: Its Development, Problems and Prospects* (London, Hutchinson, 1969), p. 188, respectively.
10. 'The Soft Pink Palms', *Présence Africaine*, viii–x, p. 113.
11. 'Book Publishing in Nigeria', *Africa Report*, April 1966, p. 57.
12. 'Nigeria in World Politics', *Présence Africaine*, xxxii–xxxiii, pp. 19–30.
13. See, for example, the repressive measures agreed on by the Prime Minister and the regional premiers in 1964 and discussed by Schwarz, op. cit., pp. 124–7.
14. 'The Novels of Disillusion', *The Journal of Commonwealth Literature*, January 1969.
15. Bernth Lindfors, 'Achebe on Commitment and African Writers', *Africa Report*, March 1970, p. 16.
16. See 'Militarism in Africa', *New Left Review*, July/August 1966.
17. 'A Relevant Art: Paddy Kitchen Talks to Chinua Achebe', *The Times Educational Supplement*, 14 April 1972, p. 19.

The Blind Men
and the Elephant

Bernth Lindfors

There is a famous story about six blind men encountering an elephant for the first time. Each man, seizing on the single feature of the animal which he happened to have touched first, and being incapable of seeing it whole, loudly maintained his limited opinion on the nature of the beast. The elephant was variously like a wall, a spear, a snake, a tree, a fan or a rope, depending on whether the blind men had first grasped the creature's side, tusk, trunk, knee, ear, or tail.[1]

I have referred to this fable because I believe it epitomises the problem of every critic who is confronted with a new work of art, especially one which comes out of a culture different from his own. It is impossible for him to see the thing whole. He may inspect it with the greatest curiosity and scholarly care, counting its parts, studying its structure, analysing its texture, probing its private recesses, measuring its real and symbolic dimensions, and trying to weigh its ultimate significance, but he will never master all its complexity, never understand everything that makes it live and move as an independent artistic creation. He simply cannot help but perceive it from his own limited point of view which has been conditioned by his previous cultural experiences. In a desperate effort to make some sense of unfamiliar lines and contours he may resort to comparisons with other forms he knows quite well, drawing parallels where oblique coincidences happen to intersect. The elephant thus becomes a wall, a spear, a snake, a tree, a fan, a rope. And the blind men bicker about the accuracy of their perceptions while truth stands huge and unrecognised in their midst.

The native critic, it has been argued, is better equipped than anyone else to appreciate the creative genius of his own culture. He is the only one who can grab the elephant by the tail and still look him straight in the eye. He is able to achieve this partly because he was born and bred closest to the beastly truth and partly because his upbringing has endowed him with superior insight into the workings of his society, the ground upon which this truth stands. Yet it would seem obvious that anyone so close to what he is viewing would have trouble viewing it in a larger context and assessing it with the kind of dispassionate objectivity that rational aesthetic evaluation requires. Indeed, if all interpretation were left to native critics, truth might be sought principally on a local level, its universal dimensions all but forgotten. Common sense just does not allow a single tribe of critics to claim a monopoly on clear vision. Every individual will have his blind spots, and some critics – native as well as foreign – will be much blinder than others.

This is why any literature needs all the criticism it can get. Only by glimpsing truth from a variety of perspectives are we able to comprehend its complexities and ambiguities. Only by comparing different views of the same subject can we arrive at a valid conception of what it really looks like. If we choose to stand still and see everything through rose-coloured spectacles, we will have a narrow, tainted vision of reality. Our image of the elephant will be incomplete and distorted by our bias.

If we could learn to accept the fact that no individual – not even the author himself – is capable of telling the whole truth and nothing but the truth about a literary work, we would then be in a better position to evaluate the contribution a critic makes to our understanding of that work. We would not expect perfection, for we would realise that literary criticism is a fickle and uncertain art in which no-one has the final word. There are never any right or wrong answers as in elementary mathematics or physics; there are only good and bad arguments based on different interpretations of the same data.

The critic who ventures to criticise other critics must therefore not only be aware of his own perceptual limitations and guard against acute astigmatism and myopia, but he must also take pains to build a sound case for his particular point of view. It is not enough for him to swagger and shout insults at everyone who sees things differently from him. He must be sure of his footing before he casts his spear, and he must aim carefully if he wants to hit his target squarely. Above all, he must refrain from launching irrelevant personal attacks for his quarrel is not with men but with their ideas. One cannot restore a blind man's vision by flogging him.

To illustrate polar extremes of good and bad metacriticism (defined here as criticism of literary criticism) one need look no farther than *African Literature Today*, No. 5. I will select two articles, both of which happen to challenge views I expressed in earlier issues of the same journal. Ernest Emenyonu, in a provacative essay entitled 'African Literature: What does it take to be its critic?' (pp. 1-11), takes me to task for having a low opinion of Cyprian Ekwensi's art,[2] and Gareth Griffiths, in 'Language and Action in the Novels of Chinua Achebe' (pp. 88–105), questions my assertions about Achebe's use of proverbs.[3] Let us look at Emenyonu's complaints first.

Emenyonu obviously admires Ekwensi both as a literary artist and as a man. He knows him personally, has interviewed him extensively about his life and writings, and is convinced that 'both the characters and settings of his novels are truly African' (p. 7). He also seems persuaded that if I and other 'Western critics' only knew Ekwensi personally, would take the trouble to interview him extensively about his life and writings, and would try to become acquainted with the diverse African peoples and places upon which he bases his novels, then we too would be genuinely impressed with his literary genius. Indeed, until we are willing to make this investment in intimacy, we are incapable of judging him fairly for 'even well-intentioned minds' will be misled by 'inadequate information' (p. 4). Any of Ekwensi's close friends and associates would presumably be a better critic of his works than a total stranger who has never met him socially. To bolster his argument, Emenyonu offers bits and pieces of biographical data which are intended to help us understand and appreciate Ekwensi's craftsmanship. Some of this information can be found on dust jackets of Ekwensi's novels and would be very difficult for anyone remotely interested in his work to overlook. The fact that Ekwensi has had a varied career as a 'teacher, a journalist, a forestry officer, a pharmacist, a broad-caster, a features producer, a film writer, a dramatist, a national director of Information Services, head of a national broadcasting corporation, and a diplomat' is too well known to bear repeating, but the sequence in which he held these jobs while developing as a writer is, as Emenyonu rightly maintains, of vital importance to any investigation of his literary evolution. It therefore seems odd that Emenyonu should reject my attempts 'to prove something about the gap between Ekwensi's publication dates and the actual dates when the author wrote the works', (p. 6). I was not, as he states later, 'trying to assess Ekwensi's artistic growth from the chronological order of the publication of his works' (p. 7) but rather from the chronological order in which the works were *written*. In other words, I was attempting to do precisely what Emenyonu himself insists the responsible critic must do: establish a factual basis for generalisations about an author's development. It is true I had no way of knowing that 'the raw materials for *People of the City* had been collected as far back as 1947' (p. 7),[4] but I knew from delving into Ekwensi's background that the book had been written on a brief boat trip to England. However, according to three printed sources based on early interviews with the author,[5] this trip took place in 1951, not 1953 as Emenyonu claims! If Emenyonu is so intent on setting the biographical record straight, one wishes he would make an effort to verify the 'facts' he collected from Mr Ekwensi.

Another surprising inconsistency in Emenyonu's argument is his unwillingness to accept certain kinds of biographical evidence. That Ekwensi has been influenced by many types of Western literature is a fact that even Ekwensi himself would not dispute. Indeed, in 1964 he published an autobiographical essay entitled 'Literary Influences on a Young Nigerian' (*Times Literary Supplement*, 4 June 1964, pp. 475–6) in which he cited not less than 20 Western writers who had made some impact on him. In interviews he has mentioned still others as being 'always present in my imagination when I write'.[6] It therefore seems very peculiar that my efforts to document the extent of Ekwensi's debt to certain of these sources should be treated by Emenyonu with scornful sarcasm. Why are some well-established biographical facts admissible and others not?

Emenyonu would have us believe that

> *the only thing that should be known* about Ekwensi in this regard is that he had an early overpowering and almost compulsive interest in reading, especially fiction. So possessed was Ekwensi by this trait that even while his teachers were solving mathematical equations on the blackboard, Ekwensi was preoccupied with novels hidden between his legs beneath his desk. (p. 6. Italics mine)

If this interesting bit of gossip is truly the 'only thing that should be known' about Ekwensi's reading habits, why should anyone do any further research on the subject? Emenyonu seems to want to set rigid limits on certain kinds of biographical inquiry even while demanding that critics do their utmost to learn everything there is to know about the life and times of the author.

Curiously enough, some of the statements Emenyonu makes do more to support my contentions about Ekwensi than they do to refute them. For instance, his remark that 'any other West African who went through the unfortunately British dominated educational system read virtually the same titles as Ekwensi' (p. 6), reveals that Ekwensi was more profoundly influenced by certain books than were his contemporaries who had equal access to them. Otherwise, why would not more authors in British West Africa have written like Rider Haggard, Robert Louis Stevenson and Edgar Wallace? Why was Ekwensi the only one who produced juvenile adventure fiction of this indelible stamp? The answer seems to be that the others outgrew their interest in popular schoolboy classics while Ekwensi was still strongly under their spell, at least in the earliest phase of his career. There may be better explanations, but however one chooses to interpret the evidence, the fact remains that Ekwensi copied familiar foreign models which other African writers consciously or unconsciously eschewed. As an imitator of Western adolescent adventure fiction, he was unique.

What is more bizarre about Emenyonu's argument is his assumption that there is some kind of conspiracy among Western critics to denigrate the works of African authors who opt to write about 'the Africa of today, under the influence of today's economic pressures, politics, and conflict of values' (p. 6). He asserts that most Western critics prefer novels and plays set deep in the bush because these works reflect 'African primitive ways' and therefore yield the type of ethnographic and sociological data that people ignorant of contemporary African realities are invariably looking for (p. 2). If an African author defies the expectations of these prejudiced critics by writing about modern times, he is branded un-African, and if he happens to write well, he is immediately suspected of having some Western literary blood in his veins and the critics begin a frantic search for his European or American ancestors (pp. 2–3). One wonders if Emenyonu really believes in the malevolent bogeymen he has termed 'Western critics' in this imaginative scenario, of if he is merely trying to erect a racial barrier behind which he can hide suspect defensive criticism. For the strategy is quite clever. If we accept Emenyonu's premises and endorse his demonology, we are then forced to conclude (1) that any non-African who finds fault with an African literary work set in 'the Africa of today' is a narrow-minded primitivist with his heart in the jungle, and (2) any non-African who seeks to identify traces of Western influence in an African novel, play, or poem is a hardened racist incapable of explaining African literary creativity in any other way. The *deus ex machina* in this black and white morality play is of course the African critic whom Emenyonu heralds as 'more disposed to offer [his] views on an African work solely to help the reader towards gaining a *proper perspective* of the author and the realities of his work' (p. 10. Italics mine). Only a blind man of a special hue can see the elephant properly and tell the world what it really looks like!

More disturbing than the latent xenophobia underlying Emenyonu's argument is his tendency to tar many Western critics with the same brush. I cannot pretend to know as much about the motives and morals of Anne Tibble, A. G. Stock, and Austin Shelton as Emenyonu claims to know, but I can at least answer some of the charges he levels at me. First, I want to assure him that I am not hopelessly infatuated with village novels depicting 'African primitive ways'. I happen to think that the urban novels of Soyinka, Armah, and Awoonor are among the best to have come out of Africa; I prize them not because they are 'modern' in setting, theme, and technique, but because they are extraordinarily perceptive and beautifully written. I admire Achebe's rural novels for the same reason: they are elegant works of art. Secondly, my interest in African literature is more literary than anthropological, sociological, or racialistic. I do not particularly care what Africans choose to write about so long as they write well. Thirdly, I do not believe that 'a Peace Corps sojourn, a spell of field work in Africa, a conference on African literature, a graduate student-ship in African literature in a Western university, any of these is enough to qualify one as an authority on African literature' (p. 10). Nor do I believe that 'African literature in all its ramifications represents a mere appendage to British or French literature since most of the African writers write chiefly in English or French' (p. 1). I am sure these notions are as repugnant to me as they are to Emenyonu. Finally, my effort to detect foreign (*and native*!) influences on Ekwensi's writing was not a back-handed manoeuver to explain away his successes but a straight-forward attempt to account for his failures. I sincerely doubt that I will think more highly of Ekwensi as a literary artist 'as soon as [he] writes a novel about black magic, ritual, medicine men, mud and thatched huts, banana leaves, palm trees and rolling rivers' (pp. 6–7). After all, Ekwensi tried this years ago in at least two of his school readers – *Juju Rock* and *The Leopard's Claw* – and in sections of *Jagua Nana*.

All these points would have been clear to Emenyonu if he had been able to suppress his fears about Western critics plotting the overthrow of modern African literature or if he had simply known my critical writings better. Why should the courtesy of elementary biographical research be extended only to creative writers and not to critics?

One legitimate answer to this question is that biographical research really doesn't matter at all because it is totally irrelevant to literary evaluation. A writer must be judged by what he writes, not by how he lives. Interviews and other forms of biographical inquiry may be interesting ways to collect personal information about an author but they are not substitutes for intelligent appraisal of his works. This applies to novelists as well as critics. The fact that Ekwensi was a poor student of mathematics does not make him a great writer. The fact that he has had a diversified career does not guarantee that his novels will be successful. Although we cannot prevent fascinating personal revelations from conditioning our attitude towards an artist, we should never allow them to determine our response to his art. Literary biography must not usurp the function of literary criticism.

Following this train of thought, one is tempted to go a step further and postulate that the least reliable critics are likely to be those who know an author personally, for their feelings towards him as a man will subvert their critical objectivity. It would be very difficult for any close friend or lifelong enemy of an artist to view his art with scholarly detachment. Even those who know him only slightly are apt to hold firm opinions about him which will colour their reactions to what he creates. This is one of the great dangers of conducting biographical research with a tape recorder. The interviewer who interrogates the author face to face is bound to come away with a vivid impression of his character and personality, and this impression will linger and influence him when he sits down to evaluate the writer's work. If we accept Emenyonu's dictum that African literature 'should be looked at objectively or not at all' (p. 10), logic dictates that we must reject all criticism by friends, acquaintances, and interviewers of African authors. *Ergo*, we must reject Emenyonu's assessment of Ekwensi.

I admit this is an extreme position and not one which I would choose to defend with my last drop of ink. I happen to believe that biographical research is a valid and useful mode of literary investigation and that interviews are essential for eliciting an author's conception of his own work. But I do not believe that biographical criticism provides all the answers to problems of literary interpretation nor that it even necessarily raises the most meaningful questions about an author and his books. For the biographical critic is as limited in vision as anyone else and as prone to see the universe from a single point of view. If he is not aware that the author he is studying is equally crippled in insight and perception, then he is likely to be rather arrogant in his critical assertions, insisting that there is only one *proper perspective* on the truth. He will not realise that he and the author are only two blind men among many who seek to explain the mystery of the elephant by viewing it from a certain angle.

Before leaving this subject, let me say that I agree with Emenyonu that too little biographical research has been done on African authors, but I am not inclined to blame this deficiency primarily on Western critics. It seems to me that African scholars are in the best position to do this type of research, especially if they share a common cultural heritage with a prominent author.

I am not arguing that critics should avoid challenging opinions with which they disagree. Critical debates are necessary not only to correct misinformation but also, more vitally, to clarify points of view which are in conflict. Metacriticism justifies itself only by contributing something new and original to literary interpretation.

An example of good metacriticism is Gareth Griffith's 'Language and Action in the Novels of Chinua Achebe' which argues that Achebe's verbal artistry is far more subtle and complex than is generally recognised, even by critics who admire his excellence as a stylist. Griffiths points out that because Achebe is a master of irony and ambiguity, one cannot accept every statement in his fiction at its face value. There are likely to be extra nuances of meaning embedded in a word, phrase, or sentence, depending on where, when, how, why, and by whom it is uttered. This is especially true of proverbs, which must be studied *in context* before their full significance can be understood and appreciated.

Griffiths therefore takes issue with my contention that Achebe's proverbs, examined in isolation, provide a 'grammar of values' by which the deeds of characters can be measured and evaluated. Griffiths insists we must watch how these proverbs operate within the larger lexicon of rhetoric built into the novels before we can attach moral meaning to them. The proverbs cannot be trusted to deliver only one message; their environment and semantic elasticity may give them strange new shapes, abnormal connotations. Moreover, Achebe himself is at pains to prove that the old 'proverbial culture itself . . . no longer provides a valid morality [because] the proverbial universe is no longer intact (p. 93) . . . the moral universe of the proverbs with its sequence of appropriate actions and responses has disintegrated along with the society which produced it' (p. 97). By employing proverbs ironically, Achebe thus reinforces a major historical point central to all his novels.

This is a persuasive argument, and I am willing to accept most of it without question. Griffiths has exposed serious limitations in my approach to Achebe's proverbs and has offered an attractive alternative mode of analysis which he demonstrates can yield significant insights into the nature of Achebe's genius as a writer. His penetrating observations on 'proverbial patterning' and aesthetic distance help to advance our understanding of the extraordinarily complex web of social and linguistic relationships that Achebe creates in his fiction. Yet I am not entirely convinced that Griffiths' analytical procedures are basically different from my own or that they always lead him in the best direction. Proverbs are perhaps too slippery to be grasped by one hand, no matter how deft and dexterous that hand might be.

In examining Achebe's proverbs out of context, I was attempting to study them as independent resonators of moral ideas which gained amplification through frequency of sounding. The more often a particular note was heard, the more important it became in the total concert of meaning Achebe was orchestrating. The context didn't matter so much as the repeated occurrence of the same sound throughout the artistic performance, because it was through constant bombardment that the composer communicated major moral ideas to his audience.

My method of analysis could hardly be called original. Anyone who has spent time tracking down 'image clusters' in a Shakespearan play, dominant symbols in a poem, or recurring motifs in a novel has done essentially the same kind of work. It involves extracting the data from the text, organising it into logical categories, and then commenting on the significance of its patterns. It is basically a deductive technique requiring that the investigator examine a large quantity of evidence before venturing to draw conclusions.

Griffiths rejects context-free proverb analysis as inadequate because it fails to consider the 'total linguistic structure' in which the proverbs are set (p. 96). He prefers a method which will take into account unstated as well as stated truths, submerged as well as surface meanings. So he chooses to scrutinise the artist's words in context to see how their significations are changed by their surroundings. He is still looking for Achebe's moral message. He is still using a deductive method. The major difference between his approach and mine is that he is trying to read Achebe's meaning from a larger 'grammar of values' imbedded in the novels.

To do this, he must examine the same proverbs that I examined and decide when Achebe is speaking straight and when he is talking through his *alter ego*, his ironic mask, or his hat. This is not an easy job, and the great virtue of Griffiths's essay is that he usually argues well and convincingly. But there are times when what he says neither invalidates nor differs much from what I said, even though he apparently thinks our statements are at odds. For instance, he objects to my classification of the proverb 'Shall we kill a snake and carry it in our hand when we have a bag for putting long things in?' as a comment or warning 'against foolish and unworthy actions'. Clearly, in the context, the proverb does not warn against foolish or unworthy actions; in fact it is used by the old man at the Umuofia Progressive Union to justify an unworthy action, or rather to justify an action which in terms of the tribal code is acceptable but in terms of the public morality to which Obi's position exposes him is a crime (pp. 97–8).

I would argue, also from the context, that the old man cites this proverb to condemn the foolishness of not approaching a fellow Umuofian for a special favour, particularly when he is in a good position to grant it. The old man wants Obi to use his influence to help find suitable employment for a 'countryman' who has just lost his job at the Post Office. It would be foolish, indeed unworthy, of the Umuofia Progressive Union *not* to appeal to Obi, their brother in the senior service, to take the small steps necessary to remedy their compatriot's misfortune. As the old man puts it in another proverb, 'that is why we say that he who has people is richer than he who has money'.[7]

Griffiths is correct to note the irony of the situation – a proverbial plea for sane, responsible action is being perverted to justify an unworthy action – but this irony is visible only to the reader, not to the loyal members of the Umuofia Progressive Union. As Griffiths himself states, the proverb recommends 'an action which in terms of the tribal code is acceptable'. We see it differently because we stand with Achebe outside the moral universe of the average urban Umuofian, savouring its paradoxical immorality. The fact that we are in a position to appreciate a new cutting edge to an old saw does not in any way hinder the saw from continuing to operate on its original plane of significance. Indeed, the kernel notion of a 'foolish and unworthy action' is amplified as much by ironic negation as by constant affirmation. The proverb still reverberates with all the appropriate thematic and moral overtones. The din is merely augmented by the mocking echo we now hear behind each articulation of the key idea. So while Griffiths is justified in calling our attention to contextual ironies which give a proverb new dimensions of meaning, he has no right to insist that we forget all the older truths it continues to convey. For these truths may endure and even prevail in the end. If *No Longer at Ease* is not a novel about foolish, unworthy actions *and their ironic consequences*, then what is it about?

Throughout his essay Griffiths pleads for recognition of the 'relativity' of proverbial wisdom, pointing out that many proverbs are capable of yielding different meanings in different siutations and that some become quite ambiguous if not absurd when undercut by deliberate irony. This is a good point, and one wishes Griffiths were willing to recognise a similar 'relativity' in literary criticism, for sometimes he begs the question of interpretation by assuming that his opinion on a controversial text is right and others are wrong. For instance, his discussion of *A Man of the People* is based on Arthur Ravenscroft's premise that Odili is an 'unreliable' hero who, in Griffiths's words,

> struggles, as far as he is able, to act up to the ideals he proposes, but despite his intentions he is betrayed time and time again into self-deception and hypocrisy. He tells his story defensively, as if half-aware of his plight, and organises his material and his comment to justify his action and its outcome. But his efforts only serve to emphasise the gap between intention and achievement. We are simultaneously made aware of the double-standards he operates when judging his own actions and those of others, and of the tragic innocence necessary to continue such self-deceptions successfully. (pp. 99–100)

Griffiths goes on to say that Achebe succeeds in creating an 'ironic novel of high distinction' by deliberately withdrawing Odili's 'capacity for honest self-appraisal' (p. 100).

This interpretation of Odili, a further elaboration of what I would term the 'Ravenscroft heresy'[8] in Achebe studies, is almost the reverse of what the author actually intended in creating his hero. If I may lapse into the somewhat uncomfortable role of biographical critic for a moment and quote what Achebe said when answering students' questions after a lecture at the University of Texas, I think the crux of the problem will be clear. Asked what his 'outlook on Odili was' and whether he intended him 'as an object of satire, even burlesque', Achebe answered

> Well, I like that young man. He was idealistic, he was naive, he was this and he was that, but I think he was also basically honest, which makes a difference. He was very honest. He knew his own shortcomings; he even knew when his motives were not very pure. This puts him in a class worthy of attention, as far as I'm concerned.[9]

Now if an artist views his hero as a very honest man who knows his own shortcomings and critics tend to see the same character as a self-deceiving anti-hero incapable of honest self-appraisal, then something must be wrong either with the artist's art or with the critics' response to it. How else can the discrepancy be explained? One could perhaps try to prove that the artist was not fully aware of what he was doing, that his conception of his hero was largely an unconscious or intuitive one, and that he actually managed to create a character more complicated and therefore far more interesting than he had intended. Or one could perhaps take the opposite tack and criticise the critics for over-reacting to particular traits or deeds of the hero and consequently misinterpreting his role in the novel. Either way the discrepancy would be accounted for as a failure of perception on someone's part. One would simply have to decide whether it was the artist or the critic who was a bit obtuse.

A reasonable alternative to this sort of exegetical witchhunt would be an approach which recognised the validity of various interpretations of the same work of art, a relative approach in matters of aesthetic discrimination. Such an alternative would acknowledge that blind men are blind in different ways and none can be expected to see much beyond what is nearest to him. The literary artist is just another interpreter of the elephant who happens to be in a position to view things from the inside. This makes his perceptions no more valid or legitimate than those of any other critic. What really count are not the reactions of a single man but the accumulated impressions of generations of visually handicapped spectators. Only then will we be able to see the truth in the largest possible perspective.

If we adopt this relative approach to literary criticism, we come to realise that the stated opinions of Achebe, Griffiths, Emenyonu, and Lindfors on a given book are of no consequence in and of themselves but that they begin to assume importance when they are in substantial agreement or disagreement with what others think and say about the same book.

The crucial points at issue become clear only through rational debate which focusses on the ideas rather than the personalities of the debaters. This is where Griffiths proves himself a better metacritic than Emenyonu. Instead of arguing *ad hominem*, Griffiths quarrels with the basic critical assumptions upon which my case rests and then offers another way of looking at the same data which is so perceptive and revealing that I am forced to admit the cogency of his point of view. Unlike other metacritics who would have us close our eyes so they can guide us, Griffiths tries to teach us a new way of seeing. He appears to realise that metacriticism, though a blind man's art, should be concerned with providing the clearest possible vision of literary realities.

The moral of this essay is: Good metacriticism emanates from the intellect, not from the spleen, and always has as its ultimate aim a true illumination of a work of art.

NOTES

1. John Godfrey Saxe, 'The Blind Men and the Elephant', *New Nation English: Book Five (B)*, ed. Etim Akaduh, *et al.* (London, Nelson, 1968), pp. 94–6.
2. For my views on Ekwensi, see 'Cyprian Ekwensi: An African Popular Novelist', *African Literature Today*, No. 3 (London, Heinemann, 1969), pp. 2–14.
3. For my views on Achebe's use of proverbs, see 'The Palm-Oil with which Achebe's Words are Eaten', *African Literature Today*, No. 1 (London, Heinemann, 1968), pp. 3–18.
4. In a recently published interview recorded in 1962 Ekwensi speaks of *People of the City* as 'a little thing I turned out based on a number of short stories I wrote for Radio Nigeria'. The 'raw materials' had thus apparently been processed at least once before Ekwensi transmuted them into a novel. See 'Cyprian Ekwensi', *African Writers Talking: A Collection of Radio Interviews*, ed. Cosmo Pieterse and Dennis Duerden (London, Heinemann; New York, Africana, 1972), p. 78.
5. *West Africa*, 21 October 1961, p. 1,157; *West African Review*, June 1956, pp. 553, 555; *Drum*, June 1952, p. 14.
6. 'Entretien avec l'ecrivain nigerien Cyprian Ekwensi', *Afrique*, No. 24, May 1963, p. 51.
7. Chinua Achebe, *No Longer at Ease* (London, Heinemann, 1960), p. 79.
8. See Arthur Ravenscroft, 'African Literature V: Novels of Disillusion', *Journal of Commonwealth Literature*, No. 6, 1969, pp. 120–3.
9. 'Interview with Chinua Achebe', *Palaver: Interviews with Five African Writers in Texas*, ed. Bernth Lindfors, *et al.* (Austin, Texas, African and Anglo-American Institute, 1972), p. 9.

Négritude and Utopianism

Frederick Ivor Case

Aimé Césaire and Léopold Sédar Senghor are indisputably the two great leaders of the Négritude movement which was born in France in the late 1930s. It is significant that both men are now politicians of some stature and that Senghor is generally considered as one of the greatest supporters of the concept of Francophonie. He has made use of his position as President of Senegal to promote the recognition of African cultural values throughout the world and is an international figure whose reputation has spread beyond the French-speaking nations.

Césaire is less well known internationally but as a Member of Parliament in Paris representing Fort-de-France and as mayor of that Martiniquan town his preoccupation with Negro-African culture is widely known in the French-speaking world.

Césaire was born in 1913 in Martinique and eventually became a student of the *Ecole Normale Supérieure,* one of the highest academic institutions in France.[1] In his poem *Return to my Native Land*[2] he proceeds to the revalorisation of Negro-African values and asserts a belief in the dignity of the black man. He counters every European and Christian denial of the Black by a brilliant reversal of prejudices:

> I declare my crimes and say that there is nothing to
>   say in my defence
> Dances. Idols. Relapses.
> I too have murdered
> God with my idleness
> my words my gestures my obscene songs
>
> I have worn parrot feathers and
> musk-cat skins
> I have worn down the patience of missionaries
> I have insulted the benefactors of humanity.

Defied Tyre. Defied Sydon.
Adored the Zambezi.
The expanse of my perversity confounds me. (*Return* . . . p. 57)

Sometimes, however, this ironic reversal is not sufficient to express his anger or indignation and he simply asserts the superior qualities of certain aspects of Negro-African culture:

> Heia for the royal Kailcedrate!
> Heia for those who have never invented anything
> those who never explored anything
> those who never tamed anything
>
> those who give themselves up to the essence of all
>   things
> ignorant of the surfaces but struck by the movement of
>   all things
> free of the desire to tame but familiar with the play
>   of the world (*Return* . . . p. 75)

It is necessary to examine these and other passages in the poem carefully since one could conclude, like Sartre in *Orphée Noir*,[3] that Négritude is a *racisme antiraciste*. Césaire is repudiating the cloak of white 'sophistication' without repudiating the white man and all his values.

One of the principal characteristics of any racism is its negative basis. It is, essentially, the negation of the humanity of a racial group and the denial of all the values of that group. Césaire's Négritude, and Senghor's also, is the affirmation of African cultural values. It is a positive expression of human dignity and pride which, of necessity, has to be preceded by a 'purification' of the harmful aspects of the Western European conditioning of the Black which has made him turn against himself. Césaire's repudiation of this conditioning is the recognition that cultural and religious values are not absolute but entirely relative. As Senghor declared in a speech before the Ghanaian Parliament in 1962:[4]

> Négritude is not even attachment to a particular race, our own, although such attachment is legitimate. Négritude is the awareness, defence and development of African cultural values. . . .
> However, the struggle for négritude must not be negation but affirmation.

Césaire recognises in his essay, *Discours sur le Colonialisme*,[5] that the principal error of the European lies in the equations:

> Christianity = Civilisation
> Paganism   = Barbarity

Everything and everyone is judged in relation to these values.

One certainly could not accuse Senghor of racism. Whilst Césaire was once a member of the French Communist Party and is still a Marxist,[6] Senghor has been Catholic for most of his life. Born in 1906, he also left his native land to further his academic education in France and was also a student at the *Ecole Normale Supérieure*.

Senghor's greatest contribution to the Négritude movement appears to have been his personal influence on Caribbean writers, the sons of a people who had for centuries been humiliated, enslaved and alienated from their culture and from themselves in the name of Western European Christianity.

Senghor's poetic work is characterised by a quiet dignity and pride, his richest verse, mostly composed to be set to traditional West African instruments, expresses his desire to return to the native village that he has left so very far behind:

Toko'Waly my uncle, do you remember those distant nights when my
    head grew heavy against the patience of your back?
Or holding me by the hand, your hand led me through the shadows
    and signs?
The fields are flowers of glowworms; the stars come to rest on the
    grass, on the trees.
All around is silence.
Only the droning scents of the bush, hives of red bees drowning the
    stridulation of the crickets
And the muffled tom-tom, the far-off breathing of the night.
                    ('For Koras and Balafong' in *Chants d'Ombre*)

Then at the end of that very beautiful poem 'Joal' which is also in the collection *Chants d'Ombre*[7] we read this striking stanza:

I remember, I remember . . .
In my head the rhythm of the tramp tramp
So wearily down the days of Europe where there comes,
Now and then a little orphaned jazz that goes sobbing,
    sobbing, sobbing.

It is particularly in this first collection of his poems that the nostalgic note is struck although it is also evident in the later collections of verse.[8]

Senghor also condemns the savagery of the European rape of Africa but acknowledges a great debt to French humanism and to the French language. His speeches and essays[9] are of great importance and interest to the student of Negro-African cultures.

What is very striking indeed in Senghor's writings is the passionate love of Africa and of France which never seem to enter into conflict. Speaking of Africa he says:

> What is forgotten is that this land was abandoned for three centuries to the bloody cupidity of slave traders; that through the murderous actions of the Whites, twenty millions of its children were deported to the West Indies and to the Americas,[10] that two hundred million died in man hunts. What is generally forgotten is that each 'benefit of colonisation' has had its reverse. (*Négritude et Humanisme.* p. 89)

In the same article, which appeared in *Présence Africaine* in 1950, he goes on to say that the West's technological contribution to Africa is of value only if the soul of the African is not altogether altered by the new exterior forces that threaten its tranquil homogeneity.

In a very famous article entitled 'French as a Language of Culture' which appeared in the November 1962 number of *Esprit*, Senghor gives five reasons why the French language is of such great importance to African writers. Firstly, he says, many of the elite think in French and speak it better than their mother tongue. Secondly, there is the richness of the French vocabulary. Thirdly, French, through its syntax, is a concise language:

> To the syntax of juxtaposition of Negro-African languages is opposed the syntax of subordination of French; to the syntax of concrete reality, that of abstract thought: in point of fact, the syntax of reason to that of emotion.[11] (*Négritude et Humanisme* p. 360)

Fourthly, the stylistic demands of the French language open new universal dimensions to the reader. It is the fifth reason that is of particular concern here, and I will quote the entire paragraph that explains it.

> Fifth reason: French Humanism. It is precisely in this elucidation, in this *re-creation*, that French Humanism consists. For man is the object of its activity. Whether it be in the case of Law, of Literature, of Art, even of Science, the distinguishing mark of French genius lies in this concern with Man. French always expresses a *moral*. This gives it its character of *universality* which counterbalances its tendency to individualism. (ibid. p. 361)

In the poem 'Prayer for Peace' dedicated to Georges and Claude Pompidou, Senghor prays for France:

> O Lord, take from my memory the France which is not
> France, mask of smallness and hatred upon the face of
> France

That mask of smallness and hatred for which I have hatred
. . . yet I may well hate Evil
For I have a great weakness for France.
Bless this people who were tied and twice able to free their
hands and proclaim the coming of the poor into the
kingdom
Who turned the slaves of the day into men free equal
fraternal
Bless these people who brought me Thy Good News, Lord,
and opened my heavy eyelids to the light of faith.

('Prayer for Peace' in *Hosties Noires*)

This poem was written in 1945 and it hardly seems that Senghor's love of France and his gratitude have altered.

Though Césaire does not insist on his love of France in his work, both he and Senghor, the Marxist and the Catholic, look forward to the day when all peoples will recognise and respect differences in culture and when all the oppressed of the world will join hands in brotherhood.

In his play *Et les Chiens se taisaient*,[12] Césaire's hero illustrates universal tolerance:

Suppose that the world were a forest. Good!
There are baobabs, flourishing oaks, black pines and
white walnuts;
I would like them all to grow, firm and strong,
different in wood, in bearing, in colour,
but equally full of sap and without one encroaching on
the other's space,
different at the base
but oh!
(Ecstatically)
may their heads join high, very high, in the ether
so as to form for all
a single roof
I say the only protective roof!

(*Et les Chiens . . .* Acte II)

It would be superfluous to quote similar sentiments expressed by Senghor since they are easily to be found in his speeches and essays.

What seems to characterise Négritude then is an assertion of African dignity, a desire to return to the cultural values which are deeply rooted in traditional religion, and the future hope of a universal brotherhood in a universal civilisation.

I will now attempt to analyse this black ideology through the application of certain concepts on African ontology discussed by Professor John Mbiti in his book *African Religions and Philosophy*.[13]

John Mbiti defines two dimensions of African reality which he calls the Sasa period and the Zamani.[14] The Sasa is the now, the immediate future, the near period of time in the past, present, and future. Zamani is the period beyond which nothing can go. It is the past incorporating the present. To illustrate this I will recall briefly Mbiti's exposition of the concept of life and death among many African peoples.

Whilst I am alive, I live in the Sasa period which will continue for me, as a living dead, even after my death. For as long as there is someone who remembers me whilst I was alive and as long as my name still evokes a real image which is neither myth nor legend, then my Sasa, my present reality, continues. I progress into the Zamani when my name no longer evokes this reality in the mind of anyone. Only then am I truly dead, and only then do I become a part of the spiritual body, which, by its progression into the Zamani, comes close to God.

Mbiti sets out to show that existence is apprehended by the African in traditional society in such a way that the immediate future is the only future perspective that exists. Consequently, in traditional religions there is no prophetism and no future paradise. For time – to use Western terms – recedes rather than progresses and the Golden Age – that era of the black man's greatness – the era of Timbuctoo and Benin, the era of the Yoruba and the Zulu, of Shango and Chaka, lies in the Zamani period. The Sasa is an ever-constant construction of the past and not of the future. Utopia exists in the past.

It is interesting that if one examines the works of Senghor and Césaire it becomes evident that they are characterised by elements peculiar to the Zamani period. The revalorisation of African artistic and humanistic values coincides inevitably with the creation of a myth superimposed on African history. It is difficult to say which comes first since revalorisation and myth are interwoven to the point of identification, one with the other.

The references in Césaire's *Return to my Native Land* to the periods of African greatness are many and there is a defiant insistence on the value of what may well be lost completely for most West Indians and for many Africans. One cannot do better than quote this very famous passage:

I refuse to pass my swellings off for authentic glories. And I laugh at my old childish imaginings.

No, we have never been amazons at the court of the King of Dahomey, nor princes of Ghana with eight hundred camels, nor doctors at Timbuctoo when Askia the Great was king, nor architects at Djenné, nor Madhis, nor warriors. We do not feel in our armpits the itch of those who once carried the lance. (*Return to my Native Land* p. 67)

Césaire's theatre[15] is placed entirely out of the context of the Caribbean of today. Of four plays he has written only one is concerned directly with a twentieth-century figure – Patrice Lumumba. The Congo is geographically very far from Martinique and from the author's socio-cultural situation in Paris. Lumumba's Congo is no nearer Césaire's Sasa than is King Christophe's Haiti.

Senghor's poems convey an attitude and an atmosphere that are different. But this *normalien* living in Paris and writing of a traditional African society is in fact looking back to what is another age and another place in terms of his evolution within the Western European world. Like so many African and Caribbean writers he is at a great distance in terms of space and time from his subject.

This brings to mind the story of Camara Laye and the composition of *L'Enfant Noir*, translated variously as *The African Child* and *The Black Child*. At the time of writing, Laye was experiencing the solitude and misery of the black worker in France.[16] He would work in the factory during the day and return alone to the Africa he was trying to recreate for himself in his cold, barren room. The result is stunning in its stark simplicity but it is the fruit of a very painful period of parturition.

Senghor, the intellectual, has long left this stage behind him. He does not battle against being an *assimilado* and accepts his cultural *métissage* and is proud of it. In an article entitled 'On the Freedom of the Soul or the Praises of Métissage' which appeared in the October 1950 issue of *Liberté de l'Esprit*, Senghor reminds us that most great civilisations have depended on the grafting of culture on culture to reach their high stage of development. Africans should therefore take advantage of this opportunity in cultural development being offered by the European colonisation of their native land. The same idea is repeated several times in his essays and speeches. In the 1956 Conference of Black Writers and Artists, held at the Sorbonne, a lively discussion developed between the Afro-Americans and Antilleans on the one hand and the Africans on the other. Here is part of Senghor's contribution to the discussion:

> So we, too, are objectively half-castes. And this is where I would quarrel with Césaire while agreeing with him. Today we are objectively half-castes . . . much of the reasoning of French Africans derives from Descartes. This is why, quite often, you don't follow us, as we don't altogether follow you, because you, like the Anglo-Saxons, are pragmatists. (Taken from *Prose and Poetry* p. 75)

However, since Senghor can declare:

> I think in French; I express myself in French better than in my mother tongue. (*Négritude et Humanisme* p. 361)

in that famous essay published in *Esprit*, he has evidently been a victim of the acculturation which appears to have been the aim of the French educational system in Africa. This cultural imperialism serves to make the victim nostalgic and sentimental about a past that still exists in the present reality of the mass of his brothers'[17]

In terms of space and time the writer is so far removed from the reality of his people that having lived in Western society and having been assimilated by its values, the African has moved out of his traditional ecological milieu, out of the socio-cultural structure of his people and he has begun to move forward in time.

This movement can best be illustrated by referring to the first novel of Olympe Bhêly-Quénum, *Un Piege sans Fin*.[18] The novel is divided into two main parts. In the first half the hero, Ahouna, is living in the village of Kiniba with his people. Apart from brief but always tragic intrusions of white colonisers or of people who have had too much contact with them, the scene is as peaceful and dignified as in Camara's novel *The African Child*. Ahouna leaves Kiniba through a series of quite unacceptable events which also, incidentally, have their origin in the South of Dahomey, that part directly under the influence of whites. Ahouna leaves his native milieu for the first time[19] travelling very far among peoples whose tongue he cannot understand and coming increasingly into contact with the techno-logical manifestations of White Power. Once he enters this world and then the structured, brutal world of the French coloniser, events seem to leap at him and he is forever trailing behind situations which overtake him in a world where eyes are rigidly fixed on a destination, in terms of space, and on an aim, in terms of time. He is totally *dépaysé*.

What I am attempting to show is that the concept of Négritude is the direct product of a successful process of acculturation undertaken by the European in Africa. It is an intellectual concept that has nothing to do with the existential reality of the mass of black men. It is the means of integrating alienated man in the security of a myth that he has created for his own benefit and for that of his social class.

The individualism peculiar to the exercise is the antithesis of the authentic cultural values of Africa where art is for the largest possible group but yet not vulgarised. The oral tradition in literature is a com-munity participatory exercise. Dance and sculpture, by their very nature, are community-oriented activities. Aesthetics for its own sake is a nonsense and absurd since man as a collective being is forever at the centre of artistic expression. The esoteric nature of Césaire's writings leaves no doubt about the individualism of his work. His intellectualisation and mythification of the black man's reality further alienate him from his brothers with whom he can feel only an intellectual solidarity.

72

The black man in the tramway, shunned by Césaire, serves as a catalyst in *Return to my Native Land* (pp. 68–70). Césaire awakens to the reality of his blackness and to the universality of his Négritude. However, his predilection for the fine French phrase, the obscure word that frequently sends even the educated reader vainly searching in his dictionary, this parade of Western European erudition that Frantz Fanon analyses so well in *Black Skin, White Masks*, serves only to remove him yet further from his people. Indeed he appears to be writing not for them but for a white public.

le bulbe tératique de la nuit, germé de nos bassesses et de nos renoncements.
(the monstrous bulb of the night, germinated from all our meanness and renunciations.) (*Return* . . . p. 42)

Passés août où les manguiers pavoisent de toutes leurs lunules, septembre l'accoucheur de cyclones, octobre le flambeur de cannes, novembre qui ronronne aux distilleries, c'était Noël qui commençait.
(August when the mango-trees sport moons: September-midwife of cyclones: October-burning sugar-cane, November which purrs in the stills. And now Christmas beginning.) (*Return* . . . p. 43)

Iles annelées, unique carêne belle
Et je te caresse de mes mains d'océan. Et je te vire
de mes paroles alizées. Et je te lèche de mes langues d'algues.
Et je te cingle hors-flibuste

O mort ton palud pâteux!
Naufrage ton enfer de débris! j'accepte!

(Ringed islands, only lovely keel
I caress you with my ocean hands. I swing you round
with my trade-wind words. I lick you with my algae tongues.
I raid you without thought of gain.

The furred swamp of death!
The fragments of shipwrecks! I accept!) (*Return* . . . p. 83)

If I have quoted more than it is customary to do it is because I feel I must substantiate the above accusation. The translators of the poem have done an excellent job and if the English does at times seem incomprehensible it is precisely because the French is similarly obscure.[20]

Both Césaire and Senghor project themselves in another country and at another period which is no longer theirs. For Senghor thinks of a way of life now lost for him among his Serere people. Césaire looks towards a traditional African life that he cannot know and towards periods of the past when Africans governed Africa and when Africans liberated themselves of a foreign yoke in Haiti. Both men are looking towards a utopian state.

I am not trying to say that Senghor and Césaire are completely oblivious to every aspect of the black man's reality. But as a map is an abstraction of a city, province or country, the economic and political awareness of problems is an intellectualisation and institutionalisation of social reality. Négritude is then a new religion of the middle-class black intellectual and as such it dulls his sense of reality. His eyes are firmly fixed on a utopian period although he can hear the cries of anguish of his brothers struggling through their present reality. But the Western-educated intellectual is also future-oriented and yet another myth is the implication that the Zamani Utopia may return, and the Utopia is the myth that the humanistic values of Négritude will prevail and that eventually, a harmonious universal civilisation will evolve, deeply impregnated with the sap of African cultural and moral values. Western philosophies – Marxist as well as Christian – have led black intellectuals to these conclusions. Angela Davis and Martin Luther King have very much in common.

Western religious philosophy has ensnared the black man into a belief in dialectical or evolutionary processes towards universal harmony where eventually he will be assimilated or integrated. But assimilated and integrated into what? If the black man does become integrated into Western European thought patterns and humanistic values, as Césaire and Senghor have been, then he becomes alienated or a man divided against himself – whichever terminology one prefers.

The concept of Négritude cannot be the answer to any situation pertaining to the reality of the black masses. It is a fine idea, useful and necessary to the cultural development of a Western-educated elite. It is also perhaps a necessary stage in a true renaissance of African culture so long devastated or bastardised by ignorance and prejudice. But at best today Négritude seems no more than yet another of Western Europe's philosophic aberrations.

NOTES

1. Among its former students are Sartre and Pompidou.
2. A. Césaire, *Return to my Native Land* (London, Penguin, 1969), trans. Anna Bostock and John Berger.
3. J.-P. Sartre, *Orphée Noir*, Preface to L. S. Senghor, *Anthologie de la nouvelle poésie nègre et malgache de langue française* (Paris, 1948).
4. Taken from, L. S. Senghor, *Prose and Poetry* (London, O.U.P., 1965), trans. John Reed and Clive Wake. This contains only selected prose works and poems.

5. A. Césaire, *Discours sur le Colonialisme* (Paris, 1955). All translations from this text are mine.

6. In Césaire's famous letter of resignation sent to Maurice Thorez, leader of the French Communist Party, in October 1956, the Martiniquan says that the struggle of colonial peoples can in no way be compared to that of the French proletariat.

7. L. S. Senghor, *Chants d'Ombre*, pp. 106–7.

8. There is one volume that contains most of Senghor's poetic work. L. S. Senghor, *Poèmes* (Paris, 1964) contains *Chants d'Ombre* (1945); *Hosties Noires* (1948); *Ethiopiques* (1956); *Nocturnes* (1961); and assorted translations of African poems.

9. Most of the major speeches and articles from 1945–63 are published in L. S. Senghor, *Négritude et Humanisme* (Paris, 1964). All translations from this volume are mine.

10. In the original text we read: 'vingt millions de ses enfants ont été déportés au S.T.O. des Iles et des Amériques'.

11. In an earlier essay (*Négritude et Humanisme*/24) published in 1939 he writes: 'L'émotion est nègre comme la raison hellène'.

12. A. Césaire, *Et les Chiens se taisaient* (Paris, 1956). All translations from this play are mine.

13. John S. Mbiti, *African Religions and Philosophy* (London, Heinemann; New York, Praeger, 1969).

14. Mbiti uses these Swahili words because their meaning is not easily expressed in English.

15. His dramatic work consists of four important but little-known plays. *Et les Chiens se taisaient; La Tragédie du roi Christophe* (Paris, 1963); *Une Saison au Congo* (Paris, 1967); *Une Tempête* (Paris, 1969).

16. For an important account of this problem read, J.-P. N'Diaye, *Négriers modernes* (Paris, 1970).

17. Fanon's speech to the Second Congress of Black Artists and Writers which was held in Rome in 1959 deals with this problem. Entitled 'On National Culture' it forms the fourth part of the book *The Wretched of the Earth* (London, MacGibbon & Kee; New York, 1968).

18. Olympe Bhêly-Quénum, *Un Piège sans fin* (Paris, 1960).

19. Ahouna does make a short journey from Kiniba to Abomey in Chapter II. On his way back he is attacked by a snake.

20. The examples were chosen from the original text: *Cahier d'un Retour au Pays natal* (Paris, 1956). There are, of course, many others. The translations are weak in parts but these and other passages are as difficult to render in English as it would be to render Gerard Manley Hopkins' poems in French.

75

L. S. Senghor:
The Mask Poems
of *Chants d'Ombre*

Jonathan Peters

Critical judgement of Léopold Senghor's poetry is fraught with a number of problems, not all of them literary. As the poet-President of Senegal there is a distinct temptation for admirers of his versatility to be overwhelming in their praise by eulogising the politician instead of judging the poet. In addition, as the most eloquent champion of Négritude there is the tendency for novitiates as well as loyal adherents of long standing to extol the leader's poetry because he is a good and faithful leader rather than because he is a good poet.

On the other hand, those who criticise Négritude as a strait-jacket in so far as it tries to impose a form and style of Negro-African writing instead of allowing the artist's imagination free rein are apt to see in Senghor's poetry nothing but propaganda and racism, or what Sartre in his celebrated essay, *Orphée noir*, written as a preface to Senghor's black poetry *Anthologie* of 1948 to as '*racisme anti-raciste*'.

These two kinds of problems – adulation and scorn – cast a shadow over assessments of the real value of Senghor's poetry but our major concern here is with the question of vehicle and tradition. Senghor writes in an adopted language, French, and has the French literary heritage as a frame of reference and as an influence on his work – witness the echoes and correspondences of other writers that critics have detected.[1] He has also studied the language and poetry of traditional African languages (notably those of Senegal) and claims these as his models as well as the work of Negro-American poets of the Negro Renaissance of the '20s. Questions of judgement thus arise, in view of these differing if not conflicting allegiances. For example, when Senghor – and Césaire, too – is criticised for being monotonous by French critics, is it because these critics have failed to appreciate the African rhythm of the poem which is monotonous only to the untrained ear that cannot distinguish subtle variations and that

76

is denied the benefit of the percussion instruments which should accompany the chanting of the poem?[2] When English-speaking Africans reject his poetry and his philosophy is it because they cannot read and speak French fluently and have to rely on imperfect translations?[3] And when Senghor sings the praise of black woman or black culture is it racism, racial pride or simply an imitation of the troubadour of his native Joal? No systematic answer to these broad questions is attempted in this limited study; rather, it is hoped that a close examination of the mask-poems of *Chants d'Ombre* – 'Femme noire', 'Masque nègre', 'Prière aux Masques', and 'Totem' – will point up the ambivalence in Senghor's aesthetic sensibility as a basis for judging his strengths and weaknesses.

The first of these – 'Black Woman' – addresses an unnamed woman, passive and gentle, with whom the speaker in the poem is in communion. Unlike the woman in an earlier poem, 'Nuit de Sine', the portrait of this woman fills the whole canvas as first her classic attributes followed by her particular features and finally her enduring universal traits are etched out. The poem opens into a sun-baked noon in summer, and the sight of this classic black woman whose form is remembered from childhood prompts the praise song that Senghor chants:

Naked woman, black woman
Clothed with your colour which is life, with your form which is beauty!
In your shadow I have grown up; the gentleness of your hands was laid
    over my eyes.
And now, high up on the sun-baked pass, at the heart of summer, at the
    heart of noon, I come upon you, my Promised Land,
And your beauty strikes me to the heart like the flash of an eagle.[4]

                                                PO 16–7 (pp. 105–6)

The first detail about this woman is that she is naked. In all Western poetry, even in the most sensual, it is unusual to find a poem praising a woman's beauty that introduces her simple nakedness as her first attribute.[5] This detail is followed by the revelation of her black colour which indicates her race and the reader realises that he is not reading a conventional poem written in the Western tradition. This realisation is quickly confirmed by the line following which celebrates her 'colour which is life', her 'form which is beauty'. Thus, without trepidation or fanfare, but rather with a quiet assurance, the first two lines of 'Black Woman' have asserted that the subject is nude and black, black the colour of life, and her figure the form of beauty. These critical standards established, less striking and more specific details follow. Always responsive to the tender, soothing hands on his brow, Senghor uses the recall of such a moment to introduce the sudden impact of the beauty of the black woman.

With the exception of the change from 'black' to 'dark' in the two middle sections, the first line of the poem becomes the opening refrain in all subsequent verse paragraphs. The surrealist imagery is sensual and daring in turn. From 'firm-fleshed ripe fruit', 'sombre raptures of black wine' and 'mouth making lyrical my mouth', the associations dilate into the 'savannah shuddering beneath the East Wind's eager caresses' and then contract to the 'carved tom-tom, taut tom-tom' muttering in a 'solemn contralto voice'. In the third verse paragraph the descriptive images are less bold. The woman is

Naked woman, dark woman
Oil that no breath ruffles, calm oil on the athlete's flanks, on the flanks
   of the Princes of Mali
Gazelle limbed in Paradise,

as Senghor prepares, at the end, to

. . . sing your beauty that passes, the form that I fix in the Eternal,
Before jealous Fate turn you to ashes to feed the roots of life.

As a rule, Senghor's most successful poems thrive on correspondences and contradictions, on ambiguity and paradox. 'Black Woman' is no exception to this rule. The provocative refrain would seem to indicate that the emotion is mere eroticism, with the celebrant poised, in Eliot's phrase, 'between the desire and the spasm'; yet in its development, even allowing for the apparent flights of fancy and fortuitousness of surrealist imagery, very little (if any) physical passion for the woman is manifested. In the second section of the poem where the images are the most sensual, no attempt is made to exploit the woman's nudity, for, excepting the reference to her mouth in 'mouth making lyrical my mouth' and 'Your solemn contralto voice' her beauty is not in any way inventoried. In the third section, only her skin, hair and eyes are mentioned, and with these, the promise of a sensually stimulating experience has been abrogated, as the poem reverts to generalities.

Does Senghor therefore fail in his attempt to sing the beauty of his black woman? If his aim is to celebrate the alluring charms of a beloved black woman, then, perhaps, he would do well to follow the example of the West Indian poet, Guy Tirolien, who utilises a similar order of imagery in 'Black Beauty' to achieve a far more erotic effect:

your breast of black satin
trembling to the gallop of your blood
leaping
your arms supple and long rippling in their sleekness

that white smile
eyes
set in a night-sky face
waken in me
this night
. . . .
dark-skinned twilights heavy with passion
. . . .
in the sweep of restless strength along your loins . . .[6]

Or else he must wait till *Chants pour Naëtt* (*Songs for Naëtt*, 1949) and the twin lyrics 'For two horns and a balafong':

She flies through the white flat lands, and patiently I take
    my aim
Giddy with desire. She takes her chances to the bush
Passion of thorns and thickets. Then I will bring her to bay in the
    chain of hours
Snuffing the soft panting of her flanks, mottled with shadow
And under the foolish Great Noon, I will twist her arms of glass.
The antelope's jubilant death rattle will intoxicate me, new palm wine
And I will drink long long the wild blood that rises to her heart
The milk blood that flows to her mouth, odours of damp earth.

Am I not the son of Dyogoye? Dyogoye the famished Lion
                                        PO 196 (No. 34)[7]

And again,

I will go leaping over the hills, defying the fear of the winds of the
    steppes
Defying the rivers, where virgin bodies drown in the lowest depths of
    their grief.
I will climb the sweet belly of the dunes and the ruddy thighs of day
To the shadowy gorges where with a sharp blow I will slay the dappled
    fawn of my dream.
                                        PO 197 (No. 35)

The central hunting metaphor exploited in these lines to represent the high-voltage charge of desire in the lover is far removed from the unimpassioned worship of the figure in 'Black Woman'.

It would however be premature to dismiss 'Black Woman' as uninspired without ascertaining what Senghor's purpose is, especially as the rejection of European standards of beauty and the life-source in favour of African models evinced in the opening lines of the poem is not accidental. Since he has deliberately chosen an African ideal of beauty, an African aesthetic is no doubt a valid frame of reference in judging the aim and, to a large extent, the achievement of the poem.

79

Comparing the function of imagery in European and African art in his essay 'L'esprit de la civilisation ou les lois de la culture' which was read at the First International Conference of Black Writers and Artists Senghor wrote:

> The African image is . . . not image-equation, but image-analogy – a surrealist image. . . . The object does not mean what it represents, but what it suggests, what it creates. . . . Every representation is an image, and the image, I repeat, is not an equation but a *symbol*, an ideogramme. Not only the image-figuration but also the substance – stone, earth, copper, gold, fibre – and even its line and colour. . . . I spoke of the surrealist image. But, as you no doubt suppose, African surrealism is different from European surrealism. European surrealism is empiric whilst African surrealism is mystical and metaphysical. Negro analogy presupposes and manifests the universe as a hierarchy of life-forces.[8]

This basis of interpretation renders the evocation of the African woman in 'Black Woman' an 'image-analogy' which is not simply the equivalent of an individual African woman but rather a symbol of whatever the figure suggests or creates in the mind of both artist and audience. The line and colour of the descriptive portrait are an ideogrammatic figuration of a mystical and metaphysical being which is projected but not named. But the question remains. What being is behind this projection that, in identifying with 'Negro analogy presupposes and manifests the universe as a hierarchy of life-forces'?

In 'Black Woman' Senghor invokes the universal black woman who has many guises in black poetry. She has been featured as a beautiful virgin of royal stock in pastoral poetry, as a suffering but steadfast Mother Africa in typically anti-slavery and anti-oppression poetry, as a voluptuous woman linked to the fertility principle in some modern poetry (including poetry of Négritude) that utilises traditional African concepts. Sometimes two or more roles are combined in a single poem. In this regard, the poet who readily comes to mind is David Diop who, in two poems – 'Afrique, à ma mère' and 'A une danseuse noire' – depicts the black woman as having many of these functions. In Senghor's poem, the images are subtly suggestive of a variety of roles, but ultimately it is the portrait of the universal woman that stands out, invested with the many attributes of various manifestations. The origin of these mythical conceptions of African woman Senghor ascribes to the transformation of a *fait économico-social* in the essay 'Eléments constitutifs d'une civilisation d'inspiration négro-africaine' presented at the Second Congress of Black Artists and Writers:

> In Black Africa, woman holds, or rather used to hold, first place, since Arabo-Berber and European influence and the influence of nomadic

civilisations have continually reduced her role. This role is explained by the agrarian character of the black world. The explanation is correct but it goes beyond that. As always, consciousness has translated socio-economic fact into myth. Because the woman is 'permanent' in the family and life-giver (*donneuse de vie*) she has been elevated as source of the life-force (*source de force vitale*) and guardian of the home, that is, repository of the past and guarantor of the clan's future.[9]

The idealisation of the black woman in traditional Africa is seen by Senghor as a parallel to that by the Negro American poets of the 'New Negro' movement. The philosophy of these poets who precede and influence poets of Négritude is outlined in another essay, 'La poésie négro-africaine'. Senghor cites Claude Mackay, Countee Cullen, Langston Hughes and Gwendolyn Bennett among the contemporary poets (1950) who embrace this concept which he summarises as follows:

These [poets] are convinced that they contribute, with the new values, a fresh sap which will make American Civilisation blossom once again. And they possess their own special cult consisting of respect and love, of desire and adoration for *Black Woman* as symbol of Négritude. This is because Woman is, more so than Man, sensitive to the mysterious currents of life and of the cosmos and more susceptible to joy and sorrow. . . . Woman is indeed symbol, as in Africa the aim is, beyond her plastic beauty (none of whose features escapes the poet) to express her spiritual wealth.[10]

Whatever spiritual wealth the woman of Senghor's poem has is expressed in images relating to the world of nature and thus to the life principle, since, in African ontology, the physical and spiritual unite in a common hierarchy. Consequently, the elemental imagery in the two middle verse paragraphs of 'Black Woman' is full of suggestions of ripeness and maturity, desire and embrace amid drumming and spiritual song, and of cosmic forces at work:

Naked woman, dark woman
Firm-fleshed ripe fruit, sombre raptures of black wine, mouth making
  lyrical my mouth
Savannah stretching to clear horizons, savannah shuddering beneath the
  East Wind's eager caresses
Carved tom-tom, taut tom-tom, muttering under the Conqueror's fingers
Your solemn contralto voice is the spiritual song of the Beloved.

Naked woman, dark woman
Oil that no breath ruffles, calm oil on the athlete's flanks, on the flanks
  of the Princes of Mali
Gazelle limbed in Paradise, pearls are stars on the night of your skin
Under the shadow of your hair, my care is lightened by the neighbouring
  suns of your eyes.

At the beginning of *Orphée noir* (*Black Orpheus*) Sartre makes the following remark about Senghor's 'Black Woman':

A black poet – unconcerned with us – whispers to the woman he loves:

Naked woman, black woman
Dressed in your color which is life . . .
Naked woman, dark woman,
Firm fleshed ripe fruit, somber ecstasies of black wine.

and our whiteness seems to us to be a strange livid varnish that keeps our skin from breathing – white tights, worn out at the elbows and knees, under which we would find real human flesh the color of black wine if we could remove them.[11]

A recent critic, S. O. Mezu, in his penetrating study on Senghor entitled *Leopold Senghor et la defense et illustration de la civilisation noire* has remarked that the poem is 'too often quoted and as badly commented upon since the majority of critics see nothing in this poem but the "special cult consisting of respect and love, of desire and adoration for *Black Woman*" '.[12] Mezu adds that Sartre's interpretation goes beyond the meaning of the superficial lines of the poem in which elements of racism are present with or without the poet's awareness. He further points out that European writers like Dante, Petrarch and Spenser, since they did not think of race in their exaltation of White Woman are not guilty of racism, concluding with a statement about the failure of the poem as an inspired work of art that celebrates Black Woman as symbol of Négritude:

The poem expresses a disincarnated emotion, an adoration without real love, a contemplation without the desire for possession, a simple eroticism. This dry desire for a generic woman indicates the lack of spontaneity and personal attachment. The writing is far from spontaneous let alone automatic. . . . This poem is neither very personal nor very inspired. It is a beautiful painting which is a trifle cold, marvellously vivid, but in which the disengaged artist has put little of himself.[13]

The problem with Mezu's critique is that it is not so much an independent analysis of the poem as an acceptance (with some reservations) of Sartre's claim of 'anti-racist racism' without allowing that the poem is inspired. It is his reluctance to credit a work that is racist-oriented with serious artistic quality that leads him to conclude that the poem is lacking in warmth and the product of a disengaged artist, while he concedes that it is a 'beautiful painting' and 'marvellously vivid'. And since Senghor's claim that African art is *engagé* is well known, the assertion that he is disengaged from the poem is as much as to say that it is not an African poem in the best tradition. The fact remains, however, that on internal evidence this is one of the least racially inspired poems of *Chants d'Ombre* if the reader makes a willing suspension of belief based on such poems as 'Snow Upon Paris' and 'Prayer to Masks', which have racist undertones, and considers 'Black Woman' on its own merits. Then he would find the poem so richly connotative that the label of racist or disengaged or uninspired becomes hasty and narrow. Indeed, a careful reading of the poem reveals that the woman being sung is, beyond the immediate profile, an exquisitely sculptured African statue carved in the 'verbal alchemy of African poems'.[14]

Apart from the parenthetic remark by Senghor in a passage already cited that in Africa Woman is a symbol whose plastic beauty is noticed in all its facets by the poet and the verbal echo in 'Carved tom-tom' within the poem itself, Senghor has a penchant for casting the black woman in many of his poems in the *immobilité mobile* of the African mask – a tendency that is particularly evident in *Chants pour Naëtt* (*Songs for Naëtt*). These songs were almost certainly inspired by an actual black woman and the following lines represent the most striking example:

Your brows have taken that Eternal stance found on the faces of statues
But there flutters about your mask the bright wing of the seamew.
It is that haunting smile, like the leitmotiv of your melodic face.
PO 179 (No. 14)

Further evidence that he identifies the living flesh of the black woman with the solid statue comes from a comparison of some of the images in the poem with a prose passage from the essay, 'L'esprit de la civilisation'. In it, Senghor, appraising a feminine statuette of the Baoulé, comments on the 'two themes of sweetness [which] sing alternately', namely, 'the ripe fruits of the breasts' as well as the fruits of the neck, knees, crest and calves; and the columns of black honey. Other particulars from a *Fang* statuette and a *Bambara* mask-antelope include fruits of breasts, navel and knees, curved cylinders of bust, legs and thighs, strophe of horns and ears and antistrophe of 'the hair of a mane arising from the imagination of the sculptor'.[15] The two alternating themes are reminiscent of the 'firm-fleshed ripe fruit' and 'sombre raptures of black wine' in 'Black Woman' and they delineate the contours of the body that are adumbrated in the poem. For their part, the images of the mask-antelope associate with the 'Gazelle limbed in Paradise', thus sanctifying the woman in her role as totem-ancestor. The apparently fortuitous imagery of the poem is in fact carefully ordered to project an archetypal being whom Senghor decides to 'fix in the Eternal,/Before jealous Fate turn you to ashes to feed the

83

roots of life'. As a poem rooted in the African poetic tradition, therefore, this comment by Senghor concerning the African aesthetic is applicable to it:

> It is first of all sensual, profoundly rooted in subjectivity; it however transcends 'the world of feelings' (*le cadre sensible*), to discover its sense and finality in the Beyond.[16]

A detailed study of 'Black Woman' in terms of Senghor's African aesthetics is of value in approaching the kindred poem 'Negro Mask'. In this poem, the identity of the figure as a mask is one of the *données* supplied in the very title. In contrast to the expectation of a frigid, immobile and lifeless piece of sculpture the poem introduces the black mask as a sleeping woman, individualised as Koumba Tam. The ambience is somewhat reminiscent of the peacefulness that informs the atmosphere of 'Night of Sine' which is placed earlier in *Songs of Shadow*:

> She sleeps peacefully in sombre purity.
> Koumba Tam sleeps. A green palm veils the fever of the hair, coppers
>   the curved forehead.
> The closed eyelids, double cups and sealed sources.
> This subtle crescent, this lip just a little blacker and thicker – from
>   which comes the smile of the privy woman?
> The patens of the cheeks and the design of the chin sing in silent accord.
> Mask's face closed to the ephemeral, without eyes, without substance
> Perfect bronze head and its patina of time
> Untainted by varnish, blush, wrinkle trace of tears or kisses
> O face as God created you even before the memory of ages
> Face of the world's dawn, do not lay yourself open like a tender pass
>   to move my flesh
> I adore you, O Beauty, with my monochord eye!
>   PO 17–18

Once again we have a carefully ordered setting, for Koumba Tam is none other than the goddess of beauty among the Serers, Senghor's own people. The tone of this poem is one of quiet adoration from which the sensuality of 'Black Woman' is virtually excluded. The preoccupation rests, instead, in the etching of the lineaments of the face of the goddess which achieve a perfect symmetry: 'the patens of the cheeks, the design of the chin sing in silent accord'.

Since the poem is dedicated to Picasso who early recognised and was influenced by black art forms, the first half of the poem emphasises the lines, curves and accents of the face of the sleeping goddess, Koumba Tam, whose features are the ultimate in perfection and grace. The transition comes when both the sleeping goddess and the human form she takes

84

crystallise into the bronze head of the mask in the form and style of God's original model created 'even before the memory of ages'. Because the mask is made of bronze that ages it is not without its 'patina of time', but it is not subject to human caresses and emotions; nevertheless the original vision of the sleeping human form has been so appealing that at the end Senghor implores the mask-goddess not to come alive and move his flesh to a purely lustful contemplation.

In his *Léopold Sédar Senghor, l'Homme et l'Oeuvre* Armant Guibert perceptively comments on the poem's architecture as it combines the social and the sacred in a 'double current'. 'Since this poem of youth', he writes,

Senghor revealed the double current which animates the African genius: on the one hand the influence of the flesh perceptible in the play of colours and forms, and, on the other, the cult of the sacred whose images are only a lining and a semblance. Starting with a sensual evocation which still throbs with a residue of life ('the fever of the hair', 'the curved forehead'), he then suggests the silence ('silent accord') and the intemporal character of the form he contemplates ('closed to the ephemeral . . . without eyes, without substance').[17]

We have already seen the 'double current' at work in 'Black Woman', where sensual images predominate. In 'Negro Mask' the emphasis is on the religious, as the poet pays humble tribute to the goddess who, reflecting the image of the original model, is 'Face of the world's dawn', and therefore already fixed in the eternal. Much of the imagery adorns the mask-goddess with an aura of divinity or with a sense of permanence as well as peace. 'Double cups' and 'the patens of the cheeks', for example, in their association with the chalice and the silver platter recall the celebration of the Eucharist, a ritualistic and symbolic re-enactment of the act of sacrifice. And sacrifice is a fundamentally integral part of African religious worship.

The paradoxes and contradistinctions of 'Negro Mask' stem from the symbiosis of three entities – woman, ancestral mask and deity – so that the figure is both human and divine, dead and alive, form and essence, bronze mask and human flesh. Woman as symbol of life-giving forces and the statue as symbol of the ancestors are here combined with a third principle, the goddess, constituting three closely associated entities in the African sensibility.

According to the ontology of animism, the whole universe is composed of vital forces forming a hierarchy in which God, the Supreme Force, is at the apex and the grain of sand or the pebble at the base. Man is the centre of this physical and spiritual universe which he bridges through the help of his ancestors who have been translated into another plane of existence. In an early essay, 'Ce que l'homme noir apporte', Senghor points to the fact that African man invests the whole cosmos with a 'human presence' which includes the tree and the pebble as well as natural phenomena and the animal world.[18]

This phenomenon explains the mutual dependence of descendant and ancestor. The ancestors occupying a higher sphere in the hierarchy may become deified as a result of a fusion – or confusion – of myth and legend. They are intercessors on behalf of the living who keep them from becoming 'perfectly dead' by proffering them libations and other forms of earthly nourishment. The gods, to the extent that they are distinguished from the ancestors, are found still higher up in the hierarchy and it is to them that sacrifice is made and not directly to God who is the source of the life-force. The gods or spirits are themselves subordinate to male Sky or Sun and female Earth whose union, symbolised in the rain and sun fertilising the earth, gave birth to the spirit-gods who are, after all, natural phenomena, animals and plants.[19]

The sculptured masks and statues are representations of the dead ancestors who are not dead, and of the spirit-gods. They are 'at the same time symbol and dwelling. They capture and make the personal felt as effective will and give rise to the *surreal*.'[20] When the wearer of the mask performs the dance of the deity whom the mask represents he takes on the power of the god, becomes the living presence of the god, thus emphasising the importance of rhythm and dance in the psychology of the African. 'Negro Mask' is thus richly connotative of the African *Weltanschauung*, of an African *Da-sein* or *Neger-sein*, to use Senghor's own phrase.[21]

In *Prayer to Masks* Senghor, as poet of Négritude, shows his concern for the white world. The title suggests that the poem is a prayer made to the gods and spirits who watch over his race. It is more than just a prayer, however, for it contains a basic statement of Senghor's poetic credo.

An obvious distinction of 'Prayer to Masks' is that unlike 'Black Woman' and 'Negro Mask' not one but several masks are involved and their summons from the four cardinal points stresses the importance of the occasion:

Black mask, red mask, you black-and-white masks
Masks of the four points from which the Spirit breathes
I greet you in silence!
        PO 23–4

Senghor scrupulously follows the alphabetic order in his salutation to the masks – 'masque *n*oir, masque *r*ouge, vous masques *b*lanc-et-noir' – as he paints them in black, red and white, the colours of traditional Africa. His greeting is a silent one of reverence in a place whose very air smacks of eternity in its isolation from all contact with the profane.

86

Although the primary intent of the invocation is a plea to the masks, something of their character is revealed in the last lines of the preliminary address which takes up half the poem:

You distill this air of eternity in which I breathe the air of my Fathers.
Masks with faces without mask, free from all dimples and wrinkles
You who have composed this portrait, this face of mine bent over the
    altar of white paper
In your own image, hear me!

In these lines is something of the paradox inherent in the African mystique, at least from a Western standpoint. In African social art the mask is a symbolic representation of the human face, which is, in Senghor's words, 'the most faithful reflection of the soul'.[22] Far from hiding or disguising the identity beyond it, the African mask reveals in its form and texture the character of the deity it represents. The sacred masks in this poem are therefore 'without mask' because they illumine the presence of the very founders of the race. There is on the one hand an image-analogy between the face of the suppliant and the sacred mask-Fathers that have modelled his face and on the other a contrast between his own face and the 'altar of white paper', which is consecrated because it is used to record the prayer to the masks.

Following the appeal for the masks' kindly audience Senghor proceeds to the prayer proper. The subsequent six lines of the poem feature Black Africa and White Europe as objective correlatives:

See the Africa of empires dying – it is the agony of a pitiful princess
And Europe too to whom we are linked by the navel.
Fix your immobile eyes on your children who receive orders
Who give away their lives like the poor man his last garment.
Let us answer 'Present!' at the rebirth of the world
As the leaven that the white flour needs.

The futures of the two continents are inextricably linked because they have the same life-line. Thus the death of Africa, the proud and pitiful princess also spells doom for Europe. The African empires which held sway up to the nineteenth century have been disintegrating under European influence and the Second World War threatens the life of Europe torn by an inward struggle, a struggle in which the black man has been called upon to sacrifice his life for peace. But after this physical death, a new world will be born in which Africa will again have a key function, 'As the leaven that the white flour needs'.

This last phrase suggests that the black man will be charged with the task of infusing a spiritual essence into a world that is for all practical purposes white – and sterile. There follows an elaboration of the black man's role in a question and answer situation followed by an affirmation of that role:

> For who will teach rhythm to the word laid low by machines and cannons
> Who will shout with joy to wake up the dead and the orphans at the dawn?
> Say, who will give back the memory of life to the man with eviscerated hopes?
> They call us cotton men, coffee men oily men
> They call us men of death.
> We are the men of the dance, whose feet regain force by drumming on the hard earth.

The implication here is that only the black man who has maintained a constant connection with the world of nature and the world of spirits can fulfil this vital task, for the white man, in his preoccupation with a machine civilisation, has brought the world to ruin by this very machine. The Negro, who has up till the present been the downtrodden of the earth will then become the hero and the apostle of the dawn of tomorrow's world, making it rise, phoenix-like, from its own ashes.

The assertion of the black man's contribution is made with full awareness of his current existential position. He has many stereotypes, all of them revealing a bias against his colour, above all, through which is forced on him a myth of inferiority. Ironically Senghor reverts to a European myth, that of the Greek Antaeus, to make his final postulate of the black man's identity as well as his role: 'We are the men of the dance, whose feet regain force by pounding on the hard earth.'

Senghor views rhythm as the corner-stone of the Negro mystique, as the essential quality that distinguishes the Negro-African culture from that of other races. The import of this is not that the Negro has a monopoly of rhythm, but that his dependence on rhythm is unique. This dependence is particularly evident when it is compared with European art which, Senghor suggests, lapsed into decadence towards the end of the nineteenth century on account of the strictures imposed by narrow and conventional rules; the Negro's contribution in the twentieth century has been to provide the young sap needed to nourish the ailing organs of European sensibility. But rhythm for Senghor not only represents forces in art but also and more significantly forces in life, since African art is a symbol of more profound realities beyond the perceived object. Not surprisingly, therefore, in one of many definitions Senghor avers that rhythm is 'flux and reflux, night and day, inspiration and expiration, death and birth.

88

Rhythm is spirituality expressed by the most material means: volume, surfaces and lines in sculpture and architecture, stresses in poetry and music, movements in the dance.'[23]

The messianic note of much Négritude poetry is present in the questions that are posed in 'Prayer to Masks'. The apocalyptic day of destruction caused by the machines of white culture is to be followed by a day of resurrection achieved through the rhythmic flow of sap from the black aesthetic. Inasmuch as rhythm is the correlative principle of death and life and similar dualities, only beings endowed with it can infuse the vital sap into the asphyxiated nerve centre of occidental civilisation. According to Senghor, the Negro reigns supreme in the domain of rhythm; consequently, it will be his duty to teach the resuscitated world the rhythm of life and to announce the Good News in the impending dawn – an honour he has by virtue of his retention of the vital link with the cosmic forces ruling the universe as he dances the dance of the world.

What Senghor seems to have done in 'Prayer to Masks' is to accept part of the Negro stereotype which he then modifies at the same time as he tacitly rejects the other half. The physical characteristics of the Negro ('cotton men coffee men oily men') which also refer to his humble or peasant status have been sublimated in 'Black Woman' and 'Negro Mask'. What cannot be accepted here is that the Negro is black, the colour of death, for in Senghor's ontology the colour, black, during this phase, symbolises life. In any event death and life are twin aspects of the same reality. In particular, in Africa 'there is no irreducible opposition between life and death'.[24] As 'men of the dance' therefore the black race engages in a dance celebrating the renewing cycle of life and death.

The tone and attitude of 'Totem' differ from those at work in the other mask-poems. From the sensuality of 'Black Woman', the worship of 'Negro Mask' and the homily of 'Prayer to Masks' all of which have a serious outlook Senghor's mood alters in 'Totem' as he speaks in a detached, ironic vein. Hitherto he has captured imaginatively the presence of the masks which disclose a reality that goes beyond the surface to the essence. Here he must hide this very presence because of his self-conscious attempt to ward off charges of barbarism by the 'civilised' races:

I must hide in the intimate depths of my veins
The Ancestor, storm-dark skinned, shot with lightning and thunder
And my guardian animal, I must hide him
Lest I smash through the boom of scandal.
He is my faithful blood and demands fidelity
Protecting my naked pride against
Myself and all the insolence of lucky races.

PO 24 (pp. 108)

In the first two mask-poems of *Songs of Shadow* Senghor crystallises the living human flesh into the statue, the mask and the mask-antelope or totem. In them he celebrates the marriage of African archetypes, creating a composite view of African thought. 'Prayer to Masks' shows him emerging as the doyen of Négritude; it is not the much altered Négritude of later years which Senghor was to define as 'the sum total of the values of the black world' but in fact 'a weapon of defence and attack and inspiration rather than an instrument of construction'.[25] The function of the totem-ancestor in African thought is well illustrated in the opening pages of Laye Camara's *L'Enfant noir* (*The Dark Child*). Senghor's 'Totem' deploys a stance of dissimulation in order to avoid scandalous gossip by uncomprehending Europeans. It is this reaction of shame that leads (in part at least) to an opposing assertion of pride in their race and its values by Césaire, Senghor, Damas and others when their self-awareness is stirred. With the exception of this mock concealment of totem and ancestor in this poem Senghor continually lays claim to the presence of the royal blood of the ancestors in his veins and throughout his poetry emphasises their influence in his changing roles of spokesman, ambassador, politician and leader. As defender of the peasant black people of royal ancestry he dwells on their nobility and courage, their purity and innocence, their wisdom and pride, thus sounding the keynote of Négritude in its unreserved glorification of the African past. In conformity with his role as peasant, however, he displays, from time to time, his barbarous accent, his pagan desires and his bewilderment in Paris where he is among people of 'lucky races'.

The paradoxes of royal peasant and naive wisdom arise out of an acceptance-rejection syndrome of Negro stereotypes which is again typical of the school of Négritude. Thus Aimé Césaire in his *Cahier* accepts, among other things, the Negro's uninventiveness in an oft-quoted passage, for although this means that he cannot lay claim to the architectural splendour of Europe, for example, he can no more be held responsible for the lethal weapons of war. Another Négritude poet, Leon Damas demands

> Give me back my black dolls
> That I may play with them
> The naive games of my instinct
> . . . .
> I am again myself
> a new self
> from what I was Yesterday
> yesterday
>   without complexity
>   yesterday[.][26]

Senghor, after an intense and sustained personal conflict returns in *Nocturnes* to the Kingdom of Childhood which he has in a sense never really left, singing his own lullaby:

I shall sleep at dawn, my pink doll in my arms
My doll with green eyes and golden, and so wonderful a tongue
Being the tongue of the poem.
PO 200 (No. 41)

The very year, 1945, that Senghor published *Chants d'Ombre* was the year that he entered fully into politics. Although the themes in his poetry remain more or less the same, there is a trend towards a more accommodating stance with reference to Europe and France, especially in his poetry which comes increasingly under the influence of his politics. Consequently, the ambivalence towards France which in effect begins in 'For Koras and Balafong' of *Chants d'Ombre* is carried through 'The Prayer for Peace' of *Hosties noires*, the epistles of *Ethiopiques* and the elegies of *Nocturnes*. All the same, in judging his poetry we should keep his politics as far as possible at a distance so as to produce valid appraisals of his work. And when we look for masters and influences in the poetic tradition, in addition to searches for imitations of a Gobineau, a Claudel or a St Jean Perse and traces of surrealism, racism or Négritude, we should not neglect to look to see if there are any on the black side of the self-admitted *métis culturel*.

NOTES

1. The most comprehensive account of these influences is chapter 10 of S. O. Mezu's excellent critique on Senghor entitled *Léopold Sédar Senghor et la défense et illustration de la civilisation noire* (Paris, Didier, 1968).
2. Senghor often indicated instrumental accompaniment for the reading of his poems, e.g., 'For Koras and Balafong'.
3. This claim is made in Senghor's 'De la négritude', *Diogène*, No. 37, 1962, p. 22.
4. Senghor, *Poèmes* (abbreviated PO in this text), (Paris, Editions du Seuil, 1964). Citations are from the English translation by Reed and Wake in *Prose and Poetry* (London, O.U.P.), referred to as PP in this article, except for 'Prayer to Masks' and 'Black Mask' which are the present writer's own rendition.
5. Cp. C. S. Lewis, *The Four Loves* (London, Fontana Books, 1963), p. 96.
6. From the translation by Norman Shapiro in *Négritude: Black Poetry from Africa and the Caribbean* (New York, October House, 1970), p. 65.

7. *Chants pour Naëtt* was included in the last volume of Senghor's poetry, *Nocturnes*, published in 1961. Quotations are from *Nocturnes* translated by Reed and Wake (London, Heinemann, 1969), pp. 34–5.
8. *Liberté I: Négritude et Humanisme* (Paris, Editions du Seuil, 1964), p. 210. The article is slightly modified and retitled 'l'esthétique négro-africaine'.
9. ibid., p. 269.
10. ibid., p. 117.
11. Quoted from *Black American Writer, Volume 2: Poetry and Drama*, edited by C. W. E. Bigsby (London, Penguin, 1969).
12. op. cit., p. 72.
13. ibid., pp. 73–4.
14. Senghor, op. cit., p. 167.
15. ibid., p. 214. For discussions of the importance of masks and statues in African society, see *inter alia* B. Holas, 'L'Imagerie rituelle on Afrique noire' and L. Marfurt, 'Les Masques africains', both in *African Arts/Arts d'Afrique*, Spring 1968, pp. 48–53 and 54–61; H. Himmelheber, 'Sculptors and Sculptures of the Dan' in *Proceedings of the First International Congress of Africanists* (Northwestern University Press, 1964), pp. 243–55 and G. Moore's 'The Theme of the Ancestors in Senghor's Poetry', *Black Orpheus*, May 1959, pp. 15–17.
16. Senghor, op. cit., p. 164.
17. In *Léopold Sédar Senghor: l'Homme et l'Oeuvre* (*Présence Africaine*, 1962).
18. Senghor, op. cit., pp. 24–5.
19. ibid., p. 267.
20. ibid., p. 34.
21. *De la négritude*, loc. cit., p. 23.
22. *Liberté I*, p. 34.
23. ibid., 211.
24. ibid., p. 114.
25. Quoted from *Prose and Poetry*, ed. Reed and Wake, p. 97.
26. Leon Damas, *Pigments*. Quoted from Senghor's *Anthologie de la nouvelle poésie nègre et malgache*, *Présence Africaine*, 1948, p. 8 (my translation). There is a double meaning to 'black dolls' suggesting a preference for black women as well as a return to childhood.

Symbol and Meaning in
The Beautyful Ones Are Not Yet Born

Kolawole Ogungbesan

A work of art should speak for itself. Yet, because the more successful it is, the more symbolic it becomes, every work of art invariably carries more than one meaning. All the great creations of literature have been symbolic, and thereby have gained in complexity, in power, in depth and in beauty. Ayi Kwei Armah's *The Beautyful Ones Are Not Yet Born* (1968) is a work whose symbolism is so dense that no one has yet succeeded in laying bare its total pattern. For this reason the criticism of the novel has not gone far beyond scratching the surface meaning. In order to understand fully the power of Armah's imagination we need to have more than scattered insights into his use of symbols or mere impressions of his novel's symbolic structure. Criticism ought to try to describe as succinctly as possible the total pattern of the symbolism which derives from the central conflict of the work and extends to every detail, enriching as well as determining the meaning of every word. A pattern is a design built up by repetition, usually repetition with a variation, which lends unity to a work of art. Pattern in the repetition of a dominant image may be seen in *The Beautyful Ones*. This image or symbol, which recurs throughout the book, is indeed a common one – life as a journey, specified here as a road journey.

The Beautyful Ones opens and closes on the road. In the beginning, a decrepit bus, bearing the man, who is fast asleep, splutters to a stop in the dark night. At the end of the book, it is early in the morning and a very new bus, bearing the inscription which gives the novel its title, takes off on its long journey and is watched by the man, who has just woken up from a long sleep, for as long as his eyes could follow. Linking the beginning of the story – which is actually the end of a journey at the end of the day – and the end of the book – which is actually the beginning of another journey at the beginning of another day – is the man on the road, walking home.

It is not accidental that Armah has painstakingly given us the speed at which everything is moving. The light in the railway office shines dully, 'like a ball whose bounce had died completely' (p. 16).[1] The handle of the useless pencil sharpener 'sped round and round with the futile freedom of a thing connected to nothing else' (p. 20). When turned on, the rusty painted fan 'travelled with such a tired slowness that it made more noise than air' (p. 23). The railway traffic remains perpetually very slow and very sparse. The novel opens on this note of speed or more correctly, lack of speed by a vehicle which should have been kept off the road:

> The light from the bus moved uncertainly down the road until finally the two vague circles caught some indistinct object on the side of the road where it curved out in front. The bus had come to a stop. Its confused rattle had given place to an endless spastic shudder, as if its pieces were held together by too much rust ever to fall completely apart. (p. 1)

More important are the different speeds at which human beings are moving. When we first met the man, he was asleep in the bus. His fellow passengers were described as 'only bodies walking in their sleep' (p. 2), and Teacher called them, his fellow countrymen, 'the walking dead'. All the civil servants sat apathetically at their jobs. 'A job was a job. It did not matter at all that nothing was done on most jobs' (p. 183). Yet, they generated their own motion and, together with water from the nearby sea, helped to make the atmosphere in the office uncomfortably steamy. 'Everybody seemed to sweat a lot, not from the exertion of their jobs, but from some kind of inner struggle that was always going on' (p. 23). Then at 4.30 p.m. every day, the fan would stop its lazy movement and the apathetic workers would hit the road:

> With a hurry that was still instinctive after so many years of disappointment and so much knowledge of futility, the clerks put away the things they called work and made for the door. What did they think they were hurrying to? But perhaps it must be said that at the moment they did not really care about having nothing worth rushing to. All they knew was what they were fleeing. (p. 30)

There is a basic pattern in these confused movements. Broadly, there are three levels of speed. First, there are the static characters such as Rama Krishna and Teacher, both of whom were metaphorically 'running' from their society. To illustrate this inversion of nature's processes, Rama even used to stand on his head for a couple of hours every day. When we first saw him, Teacher was lying naked and rigidly immobile in his bed. At the other extreme are the rich few who are running at top speed. Usually we see them in their cars. Their speed is so great that the words 'leap' and 'soar' are used to describe it. An example is Koomson, the Party man who, we are told, 'has learned to drive' (p. 68). In between are the masses of the people – walkers. Our archetypal Everyman, the man, is one of them. 'Maybe you like this crawling that we do', his aspiring wife admonishes him, 'but I am tired of it. I would like to have someone drive me where I want to go' (p. 51). Indeed, it is the man's wife who explains the guiding philosophy of the society. The man reports:

> Teacher, my wife explained to me, step by step, that life was like a lot of roads: long roads, short roads, wide and narrow, steep and level, all sorts of roads. Next, she let me know that human beings were like so many people driving their cars on all these roads. This was the point at which she told me that those who wanted to get far had to learn to drive fast. And then she asked me what name I would give to people who were afraid to drive fast, or to drive at all. I had no name to give her, but she had not finished. Accidents would happen, she told me, but the fear of accidents would never keep men from driving. (p. 68)

Here, then, is the guiding principle of life – how to 'drive'. It explains the central conflict of the novel. Driving becomes a way of coping with life in a corrupt society. The Koomsons are wealthy because they have learned to drive. The man remains poor because he refuses to drive. His wife epitomises society's love of speed: 'She would sit there, in the train, in the bus, or in the taxi, and the way she behaved, anyone seeing her for the first time then would think it was her life, this hopping into taxis and being spoken to like a great woman' (p. 166). Some, like Teacher, have given up the road altogether, turned their backs on their society, and would not even crawl. The only time he accidentally tunes to Radio Ghana, Teacher's isolation and passivity are condemned by the highlife song intoned by a chorus of voices which by its sheer number emphasise the multitude of those who feel the agony of unsuccessfully continuing to aspire after society's goals:

> Those who are blessed with the power
> And the soaring swiftness of the eagle
> And have flown before,
> Let them go.
> I will travel slowly,
> And I too will arrive. (p. 59)

The focus of all these movements is 'the gleam', much as 'material interests' is the focus of the political struggles in *Nostromo*. Here, too, as in Conrad's story, it is not easy to explain precisely what the concept stands for. The gleam represents the luxuries of life, and carries with it

95

the moral condemnation of comfort achieved at the expense of other people's hardship. As silver is the concrete symbol of material interests in *Nostromo*, here the gleam is concretised in the significantly named hotel, the Atlantic-Caprice:

> Sometimes it seemed as if the huge building had been put there for a purpose, like that of attracting to itself all the massive anger of a people in pain. But then, if there were any angry ones at all these days, they were most certainly feeling the loneliness of mourners at a festival of crazy joy. Perhaps then the purpose of this white thing was to draw onto itself the love of a people hungry for just something such as this. The gleam, in moments of honesty, had a power to produce a disturbing ambiguity within. It would be good to say that the gleam never did attract. It would be good, but it would be far from the truth. And something terrible was happening as time went on. It was getting harder to tell whether the gleam repelled more than it attracted, attracted more than it repelled, or just did both at once in one disgustingly confused feeling all the time these heavy days. (p. 12)

All roads lead to the Atlantic-Caprice. Situated on the hill, the hotel symbolises a possibility to which all may aspire, but which only a few can attain – and those inevitably by corrupt means – because their immoral society permits no alternatives. So, the disturbing ambiguity which the gleam produces in honest people is because although it is desirable as an end the means of getting to it is morally revolting. 'Only one way. There would always be only one way for the young to reach the gleam. Cutting corners, eating the fruits of fraud' (p. 112).

The other side of the coin from the Atlantic-Caprice is the Keep Your Country Clean campaign box which 'had been a gleaming white when it was first installed, and that was not so very long ago' (p. 8). Now even the lettering on it is no longer decipherable; it is covered over thickly with the juice of every imaginable kind of waste matter. This society has got its priorities wrong, for the Keep Your Country Clean campaign is dead, the Railway and Harbour Administration Block where people work to bring revenue to the country is ugly and decaying, but the Atlantic-Caprice, solely dedicated to the comfort of a few, lives on. After one of his frequent long walks, the man gazes from a bridge at a flowing stream and notices the difference between the artificial gleam prized by his society and the natural gleam:

> From the small height of the dam, the water hit the bottom of the ditch with sufficient force to eat away the soft soil down to the harder stuff beneath, exposing a bottom of smooth pebbles with the clear water now flowing over it. How long-lasting the clearness? Far out, toward the mouth of the small stream and the sea, he could see the water

already aging into the mud of its beginnings. He drew back his gaze and was satisfied with the clearness before the inevitable muddying. It was the satisfaction of a quiet attraction, not at all like the ambiguous tumult within awakened by the gleam. And yet here undoubtedly was something close enough to the gleam, this clearness, this beautiful freedom from dirt. Somehow, there seemed to be a purity and a peace here which the gleam could never bring. (p. 27)

Yet, it would be wrong, therefore, to foresake participation in society and attempt to live in nature, as in the case of the Ghanaian who had taken the foreign name of Rama Krishna as a symbol of his soul's painful longing to escape from his immediate surroundings for everything around him showed him the horrible threat of corruption. 'Everywhere he wore a symbolic evergreen and faraway look on his face, thinking of the escape from corruption and of immortality' (p. 56). He lived on meditative exercises and special diets of honey and vinegar. He went further. He lived a life of self-nourishment; refusing to corrupt himself by touching any woman, he saved his semen to rejuvenate his brain by standing on his head for some minutes every night and every morning. When he died, very young, of consumption, his body inside had decayed far more than that of any living body, however old and near death.

Rama's fear of death and corruption, by isolating and immobilising him, had led to a greater decay than is natural in a human being. In order to escape from his corrupt surroundings, Rama had quit the road of life altogether, and decayed like a vegetable. It was rumoured that the disease which killed him had completely eaten up his lungs and that where his heart ought to have been there was only a living lot of worms gathered together tightly in the shape of a heart. He ought to have accepted the fact of corruption and decay as a part of life, and, from there, lived fully in order to justify his death. 'It seems to me that one ought to rejoice in the fact of death', James Baldwin has written, 'ought to decide, indeed, to *earn* one's death by confronting with passion the conundrum of life. One is responsible to life: it is the small beacon in the terrifying darkness from which we come and to which we shall return. One must negotiate this passage as nobly as possible, for the sake of those who are coming after us'.[2]

It is natural that on his way to see Teacher, the man should remember his other friend Rama Krishna. Teacher, like Rama, is fleeing from the corruption around him, but he has calmly and resignedly embraced death. When we first see him, he is in bed, naked and immobile, reading a book, *He Who Must Die*, by a Greek. 'It was the title that interested me' (p. 61), he pointedly tells the man. 'Once, he had asked whether it was true that we were merely asleep, and not just dead, never to aspire anymore'

(p. 108). Anything but demoniacal, his renunciation is more an empty retreat than a defiant surpassing. It is true that in his pessimism, he refers to Plato's cave story, but Armah's Teacher is not like Plato's philosopher who deliberately returned to tell stories of his wonderful vision to his entombed comrades. Rather, he is like Kierkeegard's despairing man who has cautiously willed not to be himself. He confesses to the man:

> I have not stopped wanting to meet the loved ones and to touch them and be touched by them. But you know that the loved ones are dead even when they walk around the earth like the living, and you know that all they want is that you throw away the thing in your mind that makes you think you are still alive, and their embrace will be a welcome unto death. . . . And so I run. I know I am nothing and will never be anything without them, but when most I wish to stop being nothing, then the desire to run back to those I have fled comes back with unbearable strength. Until I see again those loving arms outstretched, bringing me their gift of death. Then I stop and turn around and come back here, living my half-life of loneliness. (pp. 64–5)

Teacher himself realises that what he has called a half-life of loneliness is in fact death. 'I also am one of the dead people,' he says, 'the walking dead. A ghost. I died long ago. So long ago that not even the old libations of living blood will make me live again' (p. 71). Whoever renounces the chance to experience must stifle in himself the wish for it and, therefore, commits a sort of self-murder. Teacher confesses that he has chosen to be alone only because he cannot drive: 'I am just sitting here, and if you think I am happier than you driving out there, you just don't know what I feel inside' (p. 70). His isolation is not the same thing as freedom,[3] for the truest freedom is that which issues in action. To act is to be committed, and to be committed is to be in danger. But Teacher is a coward. In spite of his freedom to do what he wants, there is nothing happening around him that he wants to identify with. His nudity is not mere exhibitionism,[4] but a symbol of his moral and spiritual nakedness.

Armah's use of flashback has been criticised as lessening the tension of the novel.[5] Actually, it is justified in artistic terms, for it provides the background to Teacher's pessimism. His sensibility is dominated by the social despair of the years immediately following the Second World War. The war had caused a great dislocation in the psyches of the veterans and those they left behind. All over the land there was violence, most of it spontaneous and inexplicable, between individuals and groups. 'If that was not something entirely new, at any rate the frequency and the intensity of it were new things' (p. 74). However, these acts of violence directed outwards were but poor manifestations of the inner suffering. Many people who could not cope with the collapse of the traditional order which had been their refuge simply went mad. Many more went to the other extreme and retreated 'very quietly into a silence no one could hope to penetrate, something so deep that it swallowed completely men who had before been strong; they just plunged into this deep silence and died'. But the majority had gathered the broken pieces of themselves and their worlds and resignedly began to look for dock work 'with eyes that had gotten lost in the past or in the future, always in some faraway place and time, any faraway place and time, provided it was not the horrible now and here' (p. 76). The whole society was threatened with decay as intense and as nauseating as that of Rama Krishna. 'It was like rushing down mossy bottoms of steep gutters from the little hills with nothing to stop us. Only the gutters this time had no end, and the speed long before had become something far more than we could bear' (p. 80).

To cope with this spiritual malaise, alcohol and, even, thievery were tried, 'in the search for comforting darkness of the memory' (p. 81). But soon there was little of everything to be had and 'man would just have broken up and gone crazy then' but for Maanan who introduced *wee*. Everyone welcomed it because they felt it was the thing they should have had before. *Wee* does not blind people like alcohol and, in its after effects, is even less dangerous than beer. It takes people years beyond their old selves and makes them see so many miles beyond all the old points:

> *Wee* can make you see things that you might perhaps not really want to see. It is not a question of non-existent things being conjured up. *Wee* is not magic. It is just that all through life we protect ourselves in so many ways from so many hurtful truths just by managing to be a little blind here, a bit shortsighted there, and by squinting against the incoming light all the time. That is what the prudent call life. The destructive thing *wee* does is to lift the blindness and to let you see the whole of your life laid out in front of you. Now what you see, whether it comes up from hidden things inside your soul or from the common facts of the waking life you lead, is not false. But its truth is the deep, dangerous kind of truth that can certainly frighten you into desperate, gloomy act if the life you have been living is already of itself deeply gloomy and deeply desperate. That is the only sensible reason for fearing the thing. (p. 82)

Wee had taken Teacher beyond the outposts of social life in particular and life in general. He has been stripped of all the illusions that make life possible. 'When you can see the end of things even in their beginnings,' he tells the man, 'there's no more hope, unless you want to pretend, or forget, or get drunk or something' (p. 71). But Teacher was not the only one killed by too much consciousness. His friend, Kofi Billy, a veteran who used work as an opiate, was able to reconcile himself to the loss of one leg – until he discovered *wee* and the possibility of another world. 'I don't like it here' (p. 83), he told his two companions, Teacher and Maanan, under the influence of *wee*. 'I see a long way,' he continued in his sub-conscious yearning for another world, 'and it is full of people going so far into the distance that I see them all like bubbles joined together. They are going, just going, and I am only one. It is not at all possible to come out and see where we are going. I am just going' (p. 86–7).

Kofi Billy, like the vast majority of his society, was on the broad path that leadeth to destruction. His ability, under the influence of *wee*, to see a long way intensified his despair that he might be vegetating. When asked, 'Shall we go?' he replied, 'Can we go?' (p. 87). Then he went and hid from the world – and very shortly afterwards committed suicide by hanging himself. But Kofi's anguish was not an isolated case, and there was the danger that the whole society was on the road towards self-annihilation. 'We all must have thought of things far beyond this place and time, far beyond life itself,' Teacher recollected. 'I do not know why we did not all go' (p. 91).

The first signs of salvation came from men who had travelled beyond their immediate confinement – mainly to the West Indies – and returned to criticise the cruelty in the society. Yet these aspirants to political leadership were too much linked to the unjust past:

> They came like men already grown fat and cynical with the eating of centuries of power they had never struggled for, old before they had even been born into power, and ready only for the grave. They were lawyers before, something grown greasy on the troubles of people who worked the land, but now they were out to be our saviours. Their brothers and their friends were merchants eating what was left in the teeth of the white men with their companies. They too came to speak to us of salvation. (pp. 94–5)

But they did not succeed for long in making the people follow them along their road of self-deception. At a time when the masses were filled with hatred and anger for their white rulers these would-be leaders were trying desperately to ape the white men. 'What they felt for their white masters and our white masters was gratitude and faith. And they had come to us at last, to lead us and to guide us to promised tomorrows' (p. 95). When, in spite of their grandiose plans to alleviate the people's suffering, nothing happened, these leaders became objects of ridicule and the people 'thought once again of new ways to make despair bearable'. Then Maanan who had introduced *wee* as a form of escape from one of despair, introduced another curative. She came to announce the arrival of a new leader. 'You people are late. You haven't seen him yet' (p. 98).

This is the background against which we must examine Armah's criticism of Nkrumah. The 'new man' had come at a time when people were disposed to give up and had invited them to try again. He had appealed to them to rescue whatever was possible of the past and turn it into a glorious future. 'The promise was so beautiful,' Teacher recollected wistfully. 'Even those who were too young to understand it all knew at last something good was being born. It was there. We were not deceived about that' (p. 100). Nkrumah had appealed to the elemental instinct within every man, the necessity for everyone to help himself without waiting to be led by others, as the former leaders were waiting to be led by the whites. 'We do not serve ourselves if we remain like insects, fascinated by the white people's power,' Nkrumah had exhorted the people. 'Let us look inward. What are we? What have we? Can we work for ourselves? To strengthen ourselves?' (p. 101). He succeeded in making even Teacher look like a believer. 'When he stopped,' recollects Teacher, 'I was ashamed and looked around to see if anybody had been watching me.' The black people, continued Nkrumah, were their own enslavers and only they could free themselves. And he invited the crowd to chant of freedom. 'The whole crowd shouted,' continues Teacher. ' I shouted, and this time I was not ashamed' (p. 101). This leader was no joker. Maanan, the mother of the race, once again became beautiful and happy. 'She was a woman in love then' (p. 102).

Yet, so much promise had soured so soon, and Nkrumah's decay had come with an 'obscene haste'. All the attack on Armah for criticising Nkrumah's politics is unjustified.[6] True, the novelist censured personal greed masquerading as socialist programmes. 'Is it always to be true that it is impossible to have things strong and at the same time beautiful? The famished men need not stay famished. But to gorge themselves in this heartbreaking way, consuming, utterly destroying the common promise in their greed, was that ever necessary?' (p. 100). But Armah's criticism of Nkrumah is more fundamental than the failure of the latter's political or social policies. Nkrumah, by appealing to the elemental in every man, had woken up the masses. 'The beauty was in the waking of the powerless' (p. 100), says Teacher. Yet, the Osagyefo had fled from the common lot by refusing to recognise his own mortality:

How could this have grown rotten with such obscene haste? Some-times I think I will understand it, when I see it as one frightened man's flight from his own death. For he was not afraid of the old ones, the jokers. They could not have come and buried him. It was his own youth that destroyed him with the powerful ghost of its promise. Had he followed the path traced out by his youth and kept to it, what would have prevented a younger man, one more like himself in the purity of his youth, from coming before him as more fit to keep to the path? A youth who could have lived the way he himself had lived at first, the way he never could have lived again when he became the old man and shiny things began to pull the tired body toward rest and toward decay. But that would have meant another kind of death for him, this death of which he had begun to walk in daily fear. And so his own end had also to be the end of all that he had begun, and if another promise comes it cannot be the continuation of the promise he held out but which he himself consumed, utterly destroyed. Perhaps it is too cruel of us to ask that those approaching the end of the cycle should accept without fear the going and coming of life and death. (p. 103)

Nkrumah's flight from mortality is equated to his flight from the common lot. 'It is possible that it is only power itself, any kind of power, that cannot speak to the powerless. It is so simple. He was good when he had to speak to us, and liked to be with us. When that ended, everything was gone' (p. 103). Absolute power had corrupted Nkrumah absolutely. Like Rama Krishna, he yearned for immortality whereas by making way for a youthful figure the original dynamism of his vison could have been maintained. The Osagyefo had refused to recognise that movement is a part of life. 'There is nothing should break the heart in the progressive movement away from the beauty of the first days. I see growth, that is all I see within my mind' (p. 72). Decay is an inevitable part of life, part of the process of growing up. What is painful in the case of Nkrumah's regime is not the movement itself, but its dizzying speed.

Nkrumah's regime is symbolised by the man-child which Aboliga the Frog showed to Teacher from his book of freaks and oddities when both of them were kids in the primary school. Within the space of seven years, the man-child had completed a life-cycle, from birth to natural death. Compared with other nations, Ghana seemed to have aged much too soon, just as the man-child in its grey old age looked more irretrievably old, far more thoroughly decayed, than any ordinary man could ever have looked. This is the significance of the filth and excrement which several critics have found as the dominant symbol in the novel,[7] and for which some have severely criticised Armah.[8] It conveys the author's feeling of nausea at how everything has journeyed precipitously on the inevitable road to decay. 'How horribly rapid everything has been, from the days when men were not ashamed to talk of souls and of suffering and of hope, to these low days of smiles that will never again be sly enough to hide the knowledge of betrayal and deceit. There is something of an irresistible horror in such quick decay' (p. 73).

Nkrumah's decay is vastly different from that of his followers, 'those who were not always there for the simple sake of the power they could find' (p. 103), but had used their power to enrich themselves. An example is Joe Koomson, for a long time a railwayman, and then a docker, doing manual labour and, like Nostromo, a man of the people. 'Blistered hands, toughened, calloused hands. A seaman's voice. Big, rough man, a man of the docks well liked by men of the docks. Doing well, the only way we do well here. Not spitting on any countryman, only the fat merchants and their lawyer brothers and Lebanese gangster friends, and that is quite all right here' (p. 104). But all this was before Koomson went to the Nkrumah Ideological Institute at Winneba. 'That is where the shit of the country is going nowadays. . . . Everybody who wants speed goes there.' (p. 104).

Joe Koomson, in search of speed, had gone to Winneba and learned to drive. We get the dizzying speed of his life, as he and his wife journey to and from the Atlantic-Caprice. 'Such a busy night, last night,' says Koomson on one occasion to the man. 'We had to go to three different nightclubs' (p. 173). His sister-in-law has journeyed to Britain on a government scholarship to study dress-making, and now 'has fallen in love with a Jaguar, and she's going to kill herself if she can't have it'. She wants Koomson to get her the foreign exchange for it, in spite of government prohibition. 'Everything is possible,' Koomson replies to the man's objections. 'It depends on the person' (p. 175).

In this life honesty does not pay. If you decide to be honest and, like the man, walk towards the gleam, 'it will be reached when you are so old you cannot taste any of it, and when you finally get to it it will not be a reward. It will be nothing but an obscene joke' (p. 114). The only way to reach the gleam is by cutting corners and taking the leap, eating the fruits of fraud: like policemen who mount road-blocks and collect bribes from drivers; like Zacharias Lagos who augmented his meagre salary of twelve pounds and ten shillings a month by selling the property of his employers; like Abednego Yamoah who sells government petrol for himself but is so clever that it is his junior workers who get sent to jail. 'That has always been the way the gleam is approached: in one bold, corrupt leap that gives the leaper the power to laugh with contempt at those of us who still plod on the daily round, stupid, honest, dull, poor, despised, afraid. We shall never arrive. Unless of course, we too take the jump' (p. 113).

Too often, the man has been described as a passive hero. But a true understanding of Armah's symbolism would show that this is not correct. The man is indeed in the middle, resisting the 'push' of his family towards corruption and Teacher's 'pull' towards isolation and despair. Unlike the rest of his countrymen, 'only bodies in their sleep', the man is fully awake to the moral alternatives in his situation. These people are not Armah's picture of the nearest thing to the unborn beautiful ones.[9] Actually, they would leap towards the gleam if they got the opportunity; it is only the man who has deliberately chosen to walk, and he suffers the anguish of all honest men caught up in an immoral situation. 'A man, even a man who has stumbled once,' he muses as he surveys his surroundings, 'ought to be able to pick himself up and hurry after those who have gone before, a man ought to be able to do that, if only for the sake of the loved ones. And the man also who in his stumbling is pressed down with burdens other than his own, he also must hurry' (p. 54). He feels keenly the reproach of his family, for amidst the seductive moral darkness in which he lives, 'he is the only thing that has no way of answering the call of the night. His eyes are hurting in their wakefulness' (p. 55).

Yet, the man's alertness never amounts to nihilism. Although he remains fully awake in the darkness, his consciousness is never as total as that of Teacher – and never as inhibiting. Having listened to his friend to whom he had gone for words of comfort, the man realises that the way of isolation is not for himself. 'You have come a long way,' he metaphorically adjures Teacher to go back; and the latter replies, 'I will leave you here then'. And the man, immediately after parting from his friend, performs what must remain as the greatest condemnation of Teacher's immobility and isolation by deliberately taking a long walk and yearning for contact with his surroundings. 'He turned right for the long walk back. . . . Inside himself the man felt a vague but intense desire, something that seemed to be pushing him into contact, any kind of contact, with anything that could give it' (p. 111).

The fundamental difference between Teacher and the man is brought out in the latter's vision when, on reaching home, he went to bed and lay beside his wife. The man saw himself, in his student days, together with a female companion – obviously his wife – leaving the dark hovels behind and walking towards the shiny towers of Legon University and the Atlantic-Caprice, 'out in the distance, far away but very clearly visible'. After he had lost his companion, snatched from him in the procession of long cars heading towards the towers, the man could not regain the original security of his simple life. 'All he can feel now is the cold, and a loneliness that corrodes his heart with despair, with the knowledge that he has lost his happy companion forever, and he cannot ever live alone (p. 118). The man's aspirations had been shared with a loved one, and while this accounts for much of his anguish it also accounts for his salvation. 'I only wish I could speak with your contempt for what goes on,' he had told Teacher. 'But I do not know whether it is envy that makes me hate what I see. I am not even sure I hate it. . . . How can I look at Oyo and I say I hate long shiny cars? How can I come back to the children and despise international schools? And then Koomson comes, and the family sees Jesus Christ in him. How can I ever feel like a human being?' (p. 109). There are many people, upright in themselves, who have thought they had no use for the sweetness, their own personal selves. 'But for such men there have been ways to get to the rotten, sweet ways. For the children' (p. 171).

Yet, Armah emphasises that family considerations cannot be a justification for compromising our morality. Concern for his family enables the man to stay firmly on the road of life, but he does not allow the claims of his loved ones to push him into taking the leap into corruption. 'Let us keep quiet and not get close to people.' Teacher counsels in despair. 'Let us keep quiet and watch.' To which the man replies: 'It is impossible for me to watch the things that go on and say nothing. I have my family. I am in the middle' (p. 109). The man is indeed in the middle of life, as opposed to Teacher and Kofi who have copped out. Yet, he refuses to be an accomplice in the corruption that is going on; within the pattern of the symbolism in the novel, he refuses to take the leap towards the gleam, like Koomson. Thus it is that when we see the man he is out there – walking. This is how best to maintain his balance. Walking thus becomes a way of coping with a life which threatens at every turn to throw one off one's moral and spiritual balance. Walking is the man's answer to the central question in the novel: 'How was it possible for a man to control himself, when the admiration of the world, the pride of his family and his own secret happiness, at least for the moment, all demanded that he lose control of himself and behave like someone he was not and would never be?' (p. 135).

The man is the exponent of the 'natural' movement of walking. His sleep in the bus conveyed the danger of withdrawal; the conductor had heaped abuses on him when he discovered that the man was a sleeper and not a watcher. Out of the bus, the man moved slowly, peering ahead in the misty dawn air. As the conductor spat on him and threatened to repeat the assault, 'he quickened his pace somewhat' (p. 8). Passing by one of the national campaign boxes, he 'walked quite slowly' and almost got knocked down by a 'fast-advancing car'. After the insults from the driver, 'the man moved a little less slowly now' (p. 11), keeping to the dark earth beside the gutter that ran the length of the road. Indeed, whenever the man quickened his step, it was in response to a threat, as when he fled from his mother-in-law, where Armah deliberately emphasises his hero as a walker:

> The man walked very quickly until he came to the nearest corner, and it was not until after he had turned that he slowed down and walked relaxedly on, free from the pressure of the old woman's measuring glance on the back of his neck. A short way up, he knocked at the door of a house standing all by itself, went in, gave the bottle of beer to his friend, and walked out again. He felt very free and very light, and walked with slow steps, enjoying his own movement. He walked close

to the large incinerator, cutting across the field in the middle of which it stood, breathing in the strong smells of burning animal skin and hair, burning paper and old ash. He did not go all the way onto the main road, but walked along the little street parallel to it. (p. 145)

The man is heroic because of the doggedness with which he clings to his honesty. His wife thinks he is crawling and wants him to take the leap. Teacher thinks the man is 'out there driving' and counsels that he should stand by and watch. He shuns both sides, continues his walk along his honest path, heroically because there is no certainty that he will be proved right. Everywhere he turns, the present condemns him by reminding him that 'only the foolish ones are those who cannot live life the way it is lived by all around them, those who will stand by the flowing river and disapprove of the current. There is no other way, and the refusal to take the leap will help absolutely no one at any time' (p. 127). What of the future? There is no certainty that things will change for the better. On the contrary:

> It would be the same for the children. They would grow up accustomed to senseless cycles, to cleaning work that left everything the same, to efforts that could only end up placing them at other people's starting points, to the damning knowledge that the race would always be won by men on stilts, and they had not been even given crutches to help them. Perhaps one of them would one day break free from the horrible cycle of the powerless. Perhaps one of them would grow up and soar upward with so much power that there would be enough left over to pull the others also up. Dreams. Dreams to break the backs of children with. Dreams to give a moment's peace to the parent who knows inside himself that things never work out that way. (p. 139)

The military coup which toppled Nkrumah seemed to indicate that things might work out that way. But the man was wide awake enough not to join the walking dead who jubilated on the streets: 'I know nothing of the men. What will I be demonstrating for?' (p. 186). After office hours, as he walked home the man felt completely apart from all that was taking place. Yet, his subconscious recognised the importance of the revolution, for when he reached home, 'like a happy man he did not climb up the four little steps onto the verandah, but leaped lightly up, thinking of youth and days in school when the sun had shone sweetly in the fields' (p. 188). This leap – the only one he took in the course of the story – almost brought him into a head-on collision with his wife who hurriedly announced the presence of Koomson, now a fugitive.

Here lies the importance of the coup. It is true that no fundamental change has taken place in the life of the nation; just a change of men, not

106

of programmes. 'A painful shrinking of the world from those days Teacher still looked back to, when the single mind was filled with the hopes of a whole people' (p. 196). Yet a fundamental change has taken place within the life of the individual. Koomson is like 'a man at his own funeral'. Like the bus conductor at the beginning of the story, he is shaken by this apparent rousing which has turned the sleepers into watchers. For the individual it is a dizzying experience. 'Here was the real change. The individual man of power now shivering, his head filled with the fear of the vengeance of those he had wronged. For him everything was going to change' (p. 191).

Koomson's escape through the latrine which he had disdained to use on an earlier occasion even to answer what he then considered 'the call of nature', is a reversal of the leap that had carried him to power. On the former occasion he had been described as 'a man who had escaped, now being brought close to all the things he had leaped beyond' (p. 158). Now the same latrine is the only means of escape, but Koomson cannot even leap out of its window, for that has been barred with upright iron bars. His escape through the hole of the lavatory seat is a parody of the leap, just as Shadwell's disappearance through the trap-door is a parody of Elisha's escape by chariot to heaven.

Now, Koomson has to walk with the man, and they both forsake the main road as they follow the narrow path of society's most ostracised worker in order to avoid detection. 'They were walking along the latrine man's circuit through life' (p. 200). During their long walk to the seaside to see the boatman, they try desperately all the time to avoid recognition. As the boatman ushers them into his decrepit house, a converted latrine, he tells Koomson: 'Ah, as for me, I have been here. This is my humble place. It is you who have come some way' (p. 204). Koomson has journeyed a long way in the course of one night. His escape by boat is a negation of his former ostentatious living; now the gleam is behind him and he is running away from it.

The man returns to shore alone on the inner tube of a motor tyre, 'moving forward in the sea with slow, comfortable movements' (p. 210). If he had hoped, by his symbolic swim, to cleanse himself of the tainted past and wake into a glorious dawn, he is soon proved wrong. After a long sleep, the first human figure he sees is a lone woman whose movement on the sand indicates that she is mad. Occasionally, she stoops to scoop a handful of sand, and rises to allow the sand to drift through her fingers, all the time muttering with all the urgency in her diseased soul: 'They have mixed it all together! Everything! They have mixed everything. And how can I find it when they have mixed it all with so many things' (p. 212). She is looking for the impossible; for the past, the present, and the future are inextricably mixed together. The loss of our illusions is the only loss from which we never recover. Maanan's madness, like Kofi Billy's suicide and Teacher's isolation, is another way out of life. As she walks away from the sun with her shadow out in front of her colouring the sand, she leaves the man 'wondering why but knowing already that he would find no answers, from her, from Teacher, or from anybody else' (p. 212).

Except, that is, from himself. So at the end, as at the beginning of the story, the man has lost his fellow travellers and is alone. Indeed, the end of the novel strongly recalls, by contrast, the beginning. Then it was dusk, now it is morning. The rusty bus and its shabbily dressed conductor have given places to 'a small bus, looking very new and neat in its green paint' and a young conductor wearing 'a pair of khaki shorts, with a light green shirt over them' (p. 213). Yet, it would be too much to read a meaning of hope into these things. 'New people, new style, old dance' (p. 185). The first bus conductor had attempted to bribe the sleeping man, thinking he was the watcher: 'Care for jot. We can share' (p. 6). The second bus conductor understood when the policeman silently raised his right hand and in a slow gesture pointed to his teeth, meaning, 'Even kola nuts can say "thanks"' (p. 214). So, he offered a bribe to the policeman, in the interests of his passengers: 'They're in a hurry . . . They want to go.' And the people themselves had not changed; if not now fast asleep they are ready to doze off; as the policeman gave the all-clear, 'the passengers leaned back in their seats and the bus took off'. The driver must have seen the man, 'the silent watcher by the roadside' (p. 214), for, 'as the bus started up the road and out of the town, he smiled and waved to the man. The man watched the bus go all the way up the road and then turn and disappear round the town boundary curve. Behind it, the green paint was brightened with an inscription carefully lettered to form an oval shape: The Beautiful Ones Are Not Yet Born'.

It is a message with which the man is very familiar. It sums up not only what he has just witnessed but the whole action of the novel and, indeed, the whole of his own life. In the centre of the oval – that is, within this corrupt society – was the man himself, represented by the single flower, 'solitary, unexplainable, and very beautiful' (p. 214). For a while after he got up to go back into the town he had left in the night, the imprint of the painted words fastened on the man's mind, 'flowing up, down, and round again' (p. 215). After some time the image itself of the flower in the middle disappeared, and was replaced by 'a single, melodious note' from the bird singing a 'strangely happy' song, perched on the roof of the school latrine. 'The man wondered what kind of bird it could be, and what its name was' (p. 215). He ought to know, for he had heard of it before, from his wife: 'The chichidodo is a bird. The chichidodo hates excrement with all its soul. But the chichidodo only feeds on maggots, and you know the maggots grow best inside the lavatory. This is the chichidodo' (p. 52). What puzzled the man was not only the nature of corruption that surrounded him but also the nature of his own honesty.

But then suddenly all his mind was consumed with thoughts of everything he was going back to – Oyo, the eyes of the children after six o'clock, the office and every day, and above all the never-ending knowledge that this aching emptiness would be all that the remainder of his own life could offer him.
He walked very slowly, going home.

These are the last words of the novel. They should be taken together with the title of the book, *The Beautyful Ones Are Not Yet Born*. This is neither a message of optimism, nor of pessimism.[10] There is no certainty that the beautiful ones *will* be born; yet the novel keeps the option open, for they *may* be born. Suffice that we know that even in such a depressing situation, it is not impossible for an honest man to keep his morality intact. Yet, there is no note of victory: the man does not feel elated for himself or for having at last won the approval of his wife for his style of living. He goes back to the centre of life, refusing to allow the last depressing situation to immobilise him. He walks slowly, going home; just as we have always seen him walking, with 'the slowness of those whose desire has nowhere to go. . . . There is no hurry. At the other end there is only the home, the land of the loved ones, and there it is only the heroes of the gleam who do not feel that they are strangers. And he has not the kind of hardness that the gleam requires' (p. 41). Honesty may be the best policy, but for this man it must for ever remain its own reward. Here, too, is a way of coping with life.

NOTES

1. All references in this essay are to the Heinemann (African Writers Series, 1968) edition of *The Beautyful Ones Are Not Yet Born*.
2. James Baldwin, *The Fire Next Time* (London, Michael Joseph, 1963), p. 99.
3. R. W. Noble, 'A Beautyful Novel', *Journal of Commonwealth Literature*, No. 9, 1970, p. 118.
4. Abiola Irele in *Okyeame*, IV: 2, June 1969, p. 126.

5. Margaret Folarin, 'An Additional Comment on Ayi Kwei Armah's *The Beautyful Ones Are Not Yet Born*', *African Literature Today*, No. 5 (London, Heinemann, 1971), p. 120.
6. E. N. Obiechina in *Okike*, No. 1, April 1971, pp. 51–3.
7. e.g. Eldred D. Jones in *African Literature Today*, No. 3 (London, Heinemann, 1969), p. 55.
8. Irele, op. cit., p. 125.
9. 'K.W.' in *West Africa*, No. 2691, 28 December 1968, p. 1541.
10. *Times Literary Supplement*, 27 March 1969, p. 333.

Kenya
and the New Jerusalem
in *A Grain of Wheat*

Leslie Monkman

The hero of James Ngugi's *Weep Not, Child,* caught in the midst of the Emergency, cries out: 'Had the country really been reduced to this? Would the Second Coming see to the destruction of all life in this world?'[1] Having emerged from the immediate horrors of the Emergency, the villagers of Ngugi's *A Grain of Wheat* have replaced Njoroge's vision of apocalyptic destruction with a more positive view of the future. Yet the novel clearly demonstrates that although a potential nation has been created, the realisation of that potential will depend on the attitudes and actions of the new country's citizens.

The epigraph of *A Grain of Wheat* introduces this emphasis on potential rather than realised achievement in biblical terms:

> Thou fool, that which thou sowest is not quickened except it die. And that which thou sowest, thou sowest not that body that shall be, but bare grain, it may chance of wheat, or of some other grain.
> *I Corinthians* 15:36[2]

The chapter from which this quotation is taken, focuses on Saint Paul's attempts to answer certain Corinthians who had questioned the resurrection of man's mortal body at the second coming. After pointing out that these men, acknowledging themselves as Christians, practise a faith rooted in the death and resurrection of Christ's mortal body, Saint Paul draws the analogy quoted by Ngugi. Here the potential for transformation is recognised in the development of a seed into a flourishing plant. Saint Paul emphasises that in Christian terms, the fulfilment of the seed's potential is achieved only through the will of God. Until that will is exercised, the seed remains at the level of potential: 'it may chance of wheat, or of some other grain'.

These transformations are related to the events of *A Grain of Wheat* when the narrator tells us:

> Waiyaki's blood contained within it a seed, a grain, which gave birth to a political party whose main strength thereafter sprang from a bond with the soil. (p. 15)

The parallel between the Kikuyu attachment to the land and the nourishment which the seed takes from the soil is evident. Yet more crucially, if God effects the transformations of nature and of the second coming, it is the people who have developed the 'grain' in Waiyaki's blood into a successful struggle for independence. Yet those same people must now nourish the seed of independence into true freedom and nationhood.

The sacrifice of Christ and the parallel sacrifices of the leaders of the independence movement were both designed to lead to rebirth, in the first case into the love of God, in the second into Uhuru. However, the Kenyan citizen has seen the betrayal of Christ's love in the conduct of the colonial Church as portrayed in *The River Between* and he must be equally aware of the possibility of failure in Uhuru if the past is recognised only in idealised views of leaders like Waiyaki and Kihika.

In his essay, 'On Heroes and Uhuru Worship', Ali Mazrui suggests that 'perhaps part of the pervasive transformation of independence [is] that there should be a revision of a nation's martyrology'.[3] The traditional pattern of immaculate hero and damned villain must be replaced by a process of 'selective memory' wherein the independent citizen attempts to honour his past without condemning any of the countrymen with whom he must build a new nation. In *A Grain of Wheat*, Ngugi extends Mazrui's analysis by demonstrating the need for a complete re-examination of traditional concepts of heroism, martyrdom, and villainy.

Following the pattern predicted by Mazrui, the villagers in Ngugi's novel have consistently elevated their heroes to the level of near-divinity. Analogies between such figures as Kihika and Christ or Moses are re-iterated over and over again. As they praise Mugo, some villagers suggest 'that in detention Mugo had been shot at and no bullet would touch his skin' (p. 246). Githua, the maimed spokesman of the villagers' hopes, epitomises the desire to re-make the past as he displays his 'Emergency-wounds' – actually incurred in a lorry accident. The narrator senses the danger and fragility in the villagers' illusions just before Mugo's confession forces them to re-examine their chosen martyrs and by implication their past:

> Like those who had come from afar to see Mugo do miracles or even speak to God, we all vaguely expected that something extraordinary

would happen. It was not exactly a happy feeling; it was more a disturbing sense of inevitable doom. (p. 246)

The villagers sense that their heroic hopes and dreams will not find fulfilment in the way they expected and a hollow optimism pervades the Independence celebrations.

Finally, the villagers realise that the possibility of rebirth and growth lies not in the elevation of heroes and condemnation of villains from the past but in the union of all men in an objective recognition of their interdependence and of their common potential for future achievement. Kihika's significance lies not just in his own actions but in the accomplishments which his actions can inspire. Ngugi develops this idea in a discussion of *The River Between*: 'An individual's importance is not only the life he leads in this world, but the effect of his work on other people after he has gone.'[4] The 'grain' in Waiyaki's blood can find fulfilment only when the people are prepared to confront their past realistically and cooperate to create a flourishing nation.

Mugo's failure to acknowledge his past left him more severely crippled than any of the other principal characters. When he finally comes to the Uhuru celebrations to make his confession, the narrator comments: 'At last the hermit had come to speak' (p. 252). Like Remi, the hero of Ngugi's play *The Black Hermit*, Mugo has tried to escape the truth of his past but must inevitably confront it directly. Remi's girl friend points out that the real hermit does not try to escape but rather 'looks for truth'[5] but for Mugo, the realisation comes too late: 'He did not want to die. He wanted to live. Mumbi had made him aware of a loss which was also a possibility.' (p. 267).

Before the Emergency, and his betrayal of Kihika, Mugo knew this world of possibility and potential:

> There was for him, then, solace in the very act of breaking the soil: to bury seeds and watch the green leaves heave and thrust themselves out of the ground, to tend plants to ripeness and then harvest. (p. 11)

This world of promise and hope degenerates into sterility and lifelessness as the grain becomes simply a particle of dust:

> Dust flew into the sky, enveloped him, then settled into his hair and clothes. Once a grain of dust went into his left eye . . . where was the fascination he used to find in the soil before the emergency. (p. 9)

The 'grain' in Waiyaki's blood serves as perfect metaphor for the bond which his successors find with the soil. Yet as Mugo finds, that bond can

113

be destroyed by isolation and self-recrimination. Saint Paul's interpretation of the events which will surround the second coming reflects the transforming power of God, but the 'glimpse of a new earth' (p. 266) which Mumbi offers to Mugo promises a world transformed by the union of men and women in a spirit of honesty and love.

This unity will not be achieved without difficulties. As the novel surveys the history of colonial Kenya, a pattern of advance and retreat becomes evident. Ignoring the warnings of Mugo wa Kibiro, the people welcome the first white missionaries and settlers but soon find that they must accept land restrictions along with the proffered religion and education. Having adopted the Christian faith, the tribe next confronts the refusal of the missionaries to reconcile such customs as that of female circumcision with the new faith. In *The River Between*, Ngugi examines the sacrifice of Waiyaki, Muthoni, and Nyambura to this conflict. Independent churches and schools rise out of such martyrdom but suffer reversals described in *Weep Not, Child* with the rise of the forest fighters. Warui recalls the glorious beginnings of the Independence movement but Gikonyo remembers the retreat:

> Long ago, Young Harry had also been detained, and sentenced to live alone on an island in the Indian Ocean for seven years. He had come back a broken man, who promised eternal cooperation with his oppressors, denouncing the Party he had helped to build. What happened yesterday could happen today. The same thing, over and over again, through history. (p. 122)

Ironically, it is the Administrative Secretary John Thompson, who recognises on the eve of his expulsion from Kenya that 'a man was born to die continually and start afresh' (p. 66). Just as the Corinthians must realise that the dead body can be resurrected by the will of God, the new citizens of Kenya must recognise that in the sins and failures of the past, the potential for positive achievement and rebirth has not been lost.

Two quotations preceding Chapter Fourteen affirm this positive vision:

> Verily, verily I say unto you. Except a corn of wheat fall into the ground and die, it abideth alone: but if it die, it bringeth forth much fruit.
> St John 12:24
> (verse underlined in black in Kihika's Bible)

> And I saw a new heaven and a new earth: for the first heaven and the first earth were passed away.
> Revelation 21:1 (p. 229)

The first passage immediately follows a statement by Jesus foretelling his own death. The second introduces Saint John the Divine's vision of the

114

new Jerusalem. Echoing the epigraph to the novel, the first passage reminds us that Mugo's solitary existence gains significance only in death. Driven by his own guilt, he has been unable to function as a meaningful part of the community. However, his confession signals a new consciousness of the need to recognise the vulnerability and interdependence of all men.

Not everyone is able to share this recognition. Karanja, having disregarded his mother's advice that 'a man who ignores the voice of his own people comes to no good end' (p. 256) is unable to begin again. He is enveloped by the void which has consumed Mugo: 'Life was empty like the dark and the mist that enclosed the world' (p. 261). Muhoya, having followed the opposite path by joining the forest fighters faces a similar reversal when he sees the former white mistress whom he had raped: 'The ghost had come to eat into his life; the cool Uhuru drink had turned insipid in his mouth' (p. 243). Yet unlike Karanja, Mugo can retreat into dangerous political pragmatism despite his awareness that 'no one will ever escape from his own actions' (p. 270).

This realisation also troubles Wambui as she worries about the justice of Mugo's trial at which she sat as judge. Both she and Warui are left 'in a solid consciousness of a terrible anti-climax' (p. 275). Warui questions his ability to continue the fight: 'Something went wrong. . . . Maybe because I am old. I am losing my sight' (p. 275). The narrator tells us that 'Warui's life was in a way, the story of the Party' (p. 22) and Mugo's confession marks the end of the party as Warui knew it. Now his successors must foster its revitalisation, its 'second coming' if the Kenyan equivalent of the new Jerusalem is to become a reality.

At the end of the novel, Mumbi reiterates the impossibility of escaping from one's actions: 'People try to rub out things, but they cannot. Things are not so easy' (p. 280). However, Mumbi and Gikonyo learn and benefit most from Mugo's martyrdom. Formerly, Mumbi's concept of heroism revolved only around figures like Kihika and Waiyaki: 'her idea of glory was something nearer the agony of Christ at the Garden of Gethsemane' (p. 102). Now in the confession of a self-described Judas, she sees a new glory and Gikonyo articulates the significance of this movement away from illusory hopes towards a realistic examination of self and society:

'He was a brave man', he said. 'He stood before much honour, praises were heaped on him. He would have become a chief. . . . Remember that few people in that meeting are fit to lift a stone against that man. Not unless I-we-too-in turn open our hearts naked for the world to look at.' (p. 265)

'Harambee' must serve not only as a political slogan but also as a description of the source of hope for the new nation. No miracles like those described by Saint Paul and Saint John will transform the country or its people. Uhuru must rest on a sympathetic understanding among all citizens and that understanding can only emerge through a balanced examination of past and present. The fruitfulness resulting from such understanding is epitomised in the new relationship of Mumbi and Gikonyo and finds perfect expression in the stool which Gikonyo will carve: 'I'll change the woman's figure. I shall carve a woman big – big with child' (p. 280).

NOTES

1. James Ngugi, *Weep Not, Child* (London, Heinemann, 1964), p. 103.
2. Ngugi, *A Grain of Wheat* (London, Heinemann, 1967), p. vii. All future citations from the novel will be taken from this edition. Page numbers will be enclosed within parentheses and inserted in the text.
3. Ali A. Mazrui, *On Heroes and Uhuru Worship* (London, Longman, 1967), p. 22.
4. Robert Serumaga, 'A Mirror of Integration: Chinua Achebe and James Ngugi', in *Protest and Conflict in African Literature*, eds. Cosmo Pieterse and Donald Munro (London, Heinemann; New York, Africana, 1969).
5. Ngugi, *The Black Hermit* (London, Heinemann, 1968), p. 52.

Jungian Archetypes and the Main Characters in Oyono's *Une Vie de Boy*

Charles E. Nnolim

I

One might well begin in the manner of T. S. Eliot by declaring that no writer is completely *original*. He owes a lot to the mind of Europe – to tradition. Startling as this assertion might seem in the criticism of an African novel, it is nevertheless true. The black writer of today owes as much to the European literary tradition as does his European counterpart. He is a product of two worlds – his African background, and the European intellectual, historical, and cultural experience. No African prose fiction is more deeply rooted in the African cultural tradition than Chinua Achebe's *Things Fall Apart*, but even here the author's training in European literature is evident. Many a critic has pointed out Okonkwo's resemblance to Aristotle's tragic hero, and the construction of the plot in the manner of a Greek tragedy. I see the work as sharing many things with the classical epic – the warrior-hero, the temporary exile of the hero, the hero's embodiment of his national cultural aspirations, the glorification of the national heritage, and so on.[1]

Oyono's *Une Vie de Boy*[2] is a novel that draws its very breath from Jungian psychology and from the Judaeo-Christian mythopoeia. Furthermore, it is one of the few examples of modern African long fictional prose that is deeply rooted in the *novel* tradition: it has deep roots in the society where the drama is enacted; it traces the growth of the protagonist, Toundi from innocence to experience; more importantly, it is preoccupied with social injustice, which forms a large part of the novel's moral realism since a large part of the interest we derive from reading *Une Vie de Boy* stems from the moral politics of it all and from the moral indignation that injustice and brutalities arouse in us.

On this note, it is very easy to see the theme of guilt looming large in the

117

novel, and to see Monsieur Moreau, the Prison Superintendent, as the vehicle of social injustice in its supreme manifestation. M. Moreau is thoroughly guilt-ridden and from the foul dust he kicks up stems a concatenation of moral abuses arising from his efforts to cover up his adultery with Madame Decazy, not with bribery or cajoling, but through his brutally sequenced, murderous tortures of the innocent witness, Joseph Toundi. We are also the indignant witnesses of other kinds of abuses in the novel – the abuse of parental authority in the intolerance of Joseph Toundi's father which drives him to Father Gilbert; the irresponsible abuse of his authority by Father Gilbert who constantly kicks Toundi in the buttocks without apparent provocation; Madame Decazy's abuse of her wifely duties in her adultery with the Prison Superintendent and in her conspiracy with him and her husband to do away with their houseboy Toundi because he knows too much; the Agricultural Engineer's immoral and frivolous involvement with a local girl, Sophie, who, in her own guilty turn, made off with his money; the Commandant's own spineless treatment of his wife when he discovered she was unfaithful, a moral cowardice that leagued him with his enemies against the innocent and vulnerable Toundi in order to protect his own tarnished reputation – all these guilt-ridden characters inhabit a society that is already poisoned by a landslide of colonial abuses. Toundi himself is not so innocent as we might have liked him to be, having abandoned the religion and culture of his fathers, into which he was soon to be fully initiated, for the paltry glitter of the white man's world.

II

It was O. Mannoni's book *Prospero and Caliban: the Psychology of Colonization* which crystallised for us the mentality of the coloniser – his tendency to project on the colonial subject all his guilt complexes, thus making him into a scapegoat. The idea of the scapegoat is as old as the Bible. Chapter 16 of *Leviticus* is the source of our current notion or interpretation of the scapegoat figure as one who is made to bear the blame for the sins of others, or one who actually suffers for others' sins. Christ is the scapegoat figure *par excellence*. The prophet Isaiah immortalises him in our imagination as one who 'hath borne our infirmities and carried our sorrow . . . wounded for our iniquities . . . bruised for our sins. . . . He shall be led as a sheep to the slaughter and shall be dumb as a lamb before his shearer, and he shall not open his mouth' (Isaiah 53: 3–7, Douay Version).

We have other scapegoat figures in Western European literature. King Oedipus exemplifies the King as sacrificial scapegoat – one to whom the corruption in the tribe is transferred and through whose sacrificial punishment the city is restored to normal. Readers of Shakespeare easily make the connection between the fate of Hamlet who resembles the Prince as sacrificial scapegoat, and that of Oedipus. 'Something is rotten in the state of Denmark' is just Shakespeare's poetic expression of the blight and plight of Oedipus' Thebes. Hamlet, like Oedipus, had to be sacrificed before the state returned to normal.

Something was also rotten in Joseph Toundi's little world. The colonial system had come to disrupt the pristine innocence of tribal life. The depraved Europeans who inhabited Toundi's world – and whose moral failings have been recounted earlier in this paper – quickly transferred the burden of their uneasy consciences to the Commandant's houseboy, Toundi. The Commandant, M. Decazy, transferred his own cowardice and inability to confront M. Moreau as a man and face his wife as a husband, to his houseboy by accusing him of being a mail-carrier and go-between. Sophie's lover, the Agricultural Engineer, fixed the blame for his own moral carelessness that made it possible for Sophie to make off with his money, on Toundi, accusing him of complicity on the trumped-up charge that Sophie was Joseph Toundi's 'fiancée-mistress'. Madame Decazy and M. Moreau first employed Toundi as a mail-carrier in their adulterous relationship, and then fearing him because he knew too much, had him jailed and tortured to the death that inevitably followed. Earlier, Joseph Toundi's father had blamed him for causing a little family misunderstanding – Toundi refused to accept this accusation and would not submit to punishment, fleeing finally to Father Gilbert.

III

In two important publications (*The Archetypes and the Collective Unconscious*, and *Psychological Reflections*) Carl Jung, who is a major influence in the growth of myth criticism, gives us the tools for exploring the darker recesses of the human psyche. Jung tells us that the *shadow*, *persona*, and *anima* are structural components of the psyche that man has inherited just as the chicken has inherited his built-in response to the hawk. In literature, the *persona*, the *anima*, and the *shadow* are projected respectively in the characters of the hero, the heroine, and the villain.

The *shadow* in Jung's theory of the psyche is the darker side of our unconscious self, the inferior and less pleasing aspect of our personality that we wish to suppress. In Shakespeare's *Othello*, Iago is the character that best fits this Jungian designation of the psyche. In *Une Vie de Boy*, M. Moreau is the *shadow*. He represents what Jung calls the invisible

119

saurian tail that man still drags behind him. M. Moreau it is who wreaks havoc on the family life of the Commandant and is the person most responsible for the destruction of Toundi. He has no redeeming features.

The *anima* is the feminine designation of the male psyche. In literature the anima-image is usually projected on women. The explanation is that every man has his own Eve within him. In Western European literature, Helen of Troy is constantly designated as the *anima* bringing war and causing suffering and confusion in the Greek world. Ophelia in *Hamlet* is also given this designation, for she becomes the bait by which Hamlet's life (although she never wished it) came to be ruined.

Madame Decazy in *Une Vie de Boy* is without question the character most fitting to be designated as the *anima*. Just as Ophelia in *Hamlet* is the unwitting siren, Madame Decazy is the witting siren of *Une Vie de Boy* – the archetypal Eve who plucks the apple in the Garden, sowing sorrow and confusion in her wake. Symbolically, it could be said that Toundi was living in paradise in the Commandant's household before the entrance of Eve – Madame Decazy. It does not take long before we discover a serpent in the Garden – Monsieur Moreau. Toundi seemingly continued to live in paradise until Madame's 'fall'. After her fall and the fear which his knowledge of it engendered in her (giving rise to her increasing hostility against his continued presence), Toundi is literally driven out of paradise and into the wilderness of life, with all its ordeals, sorrows, and brutalities. *Une Vie de Boy* thus reads like an allegory of man's betrayal of his fellow-man. The ever-fleeing Toundi becomes the archetype of the innocent scapegoat sacrificed at the altar of human insensitivity, sadism, and abuse of authority.

The *persona* (if we metaphorically take the ego or the psyche to be a coin) is the obverse of the *anima* – the image on the other side of the coin. It is the social front we display to the world. The Commandant seems to fit into this image as he presents to the world a glamorous outside (both in social position and authority) while his household burns.

Jung also has a theory of *individuation* as related to those archetypes designated as the *shadow*, the *persona*, and the *anima*. *Individuation* is a psychological growing up – the process of discovering those aspects of oneself that make one an individual different from all others. It is a 'journey' to self-recognition, to maturity. Toundi's life is a long and difficult journey from innocent, carefree youth to initiation into the existence of wile and evil in the world (exemplified in his witnessing Madame Decazy's *amours* and the rubber-bag incident), as he goes through a series of painful ordeals to a sad self-knowledge. His flight into Spanish Guinea is the archetypal search for the answer to the riddle of the Sphinx, for the mystery of that in which the purpose of man's life consists.

When he asks what may well be the most pathetic question in the literature of post-colonial Africa, one senses immediately that he has achieved both maturity and manhood through his experiences:

Brother, what are we? What are we black men who are called French?

I mentioned earlier that a genuine novel records the passage of the protagonist from the state of innocence to the state of experience, from that ignorance which is bliss to mature recognition of the actual ways of the world, from a hopeful naivety to a resigned wisdom. When Joseph Toundi says:

You see brother, ... I'm finished ... they have got me. ... My mother always used to say what my greediness would bring me to in the end. ... If I had known it would bring me to my grave. ... She was right, my mother. ... I'd made old bone if I'd been good and stayed home in the village.

it confirms me in my belief that *Une Vie de Boy* is a long prose fiction that is thoroughly rooted in the novel tradition. For the novel, in most cases, depicts a *quest*, as a young man goes out to discover his own nature and the nature of the world. This 'quest', in most cases, is a metaphorical *going forth* so that the *voyage* charts the protagonist's movement from a narrow environment (like Toundi's little village) to a broader one (the world of Father Gilbert, M. Moreau, Monsieur and Madame Decazy, the prison, and Spanish Guinea). I see Toundi's journey to maturity as twofold. It is a process of *individuation* that is both a physical journey (from the Cameroon to the Spanish Guinea), and a metaphorical one that takes him from the restricted awareness of an innocent houseboy to a sad but wider experience of the existence of evil in the world. The essential theme of the novel – of all novels – is that of education and maturation.

In view of the foregoing discussion, I suggest that an archetypal interpretation of the characters in *Une Vie de Boy* is a major vehicle of discovering the meaning of the novel. We must remember that Toundi's baptismal name is Joseph – a name that immediately calls to mind the biblical Joseph sold into slavery by his brethren who had projected onto him their own guilty feelings. Joseph is presented in the Bible as a scapegoat. Joseph Toundi comes to us revealed almost in the same light. Because he was the innocent witness of their intrigue (M. Moreau and Madame Decazy's) both conspired to do away with him. And just as the biblical Joseph's brethren deceived their father by dipping Joseph's coat in goat's blood, so Joseph Toundi's Cameroonian 'brethren' in M. Moreau's prison, deceive the white man by spattering Joseph with ox's blood, to save him from further tortures. The name symbolism is self-evident.

Joseph Toundi is also painted for us as a Christ figure – Christ, the scapegoat *par excellence*. The Catechist, as Toundi informs us himself, regarded Joseph as the new Christ. We read in Toundi's diary:

Visit from Obebe the Catechist . . . talked at length about the Passion of our Lord. Perhaps he thinks I'm a new Christ.

Many critics rightly see Oyono's *Une Vie de Boy* as a work that makes a great satiric thrust at colonial injustices in Africa. I agree. True satire such as Oyono uses as a weapon in this novel follows Addison's rule: 'to pass over a single foe to charge whole armies'. Oyono's satiric thrust is, in the main, Juvenalian rather than Horatian – there is no attempt to correct through a gentle and broadly sympathetic laughter. Rather, the satiric thrust is pointed, bitter, angry, pointing with contempt and moral indignation at the corruption of men who flaunt the hollow superiority of their race in the face of the innocent, vulnerable African. But the danger lies in critics reading *Une Vie de Boy* solely as a satire. Satire can be a potent weapon in the hands of the novelist, but when satire becomes the end rather than the means (as it is in Swift's *Gulliver's Travels* or Voltaire's *Candide*) it ceases to be a novel and becomes what Northrop Frye calls an *anatomy*.

NOTES

1. See my article, 'Achebe's *Things Fall Apart*: An Igbo National Epic', *Black Academy Review*, II, Spring and Summer 1971, pp. 55–60.
2. *Une Vie de Boy* has been translated by John Reed as *Houseboy* and appears in the African Writers Series (London, Heinemann, 1967).

COMMENTS

A Plea for Objectivity:
A Reply to Adeola James

Eustace Palmer

Mrs James's review article on my book *An Introduction to the African Novel** is a demonstration of the inanities into which the best-intentioned critics may be led when they allow themselves to be blinkered by ideological preoccupations. I hope I may be forgiven for dealing with her points in detail.

With regard to the critic's duties as enunciated by Irele, Mrs James herself agrees that I deal with the linguistic problem, so this is not a point of controversy. I also face the problem of separating 'the grain from the chaff' as even the most cursory glance at my introduction indicates. It is, however, my 'failure' to cope with the third and most important of the critic's problems – 'relating our writers' works to the whole state and condition of our people's existence. . . .' that has apparently aroused her anger. Here Mrs James has adopted a quasi-ideological posture which betrays her into illogicalities and false statements. It is quite inaccurate to suggest that critics have failed to realise that African writers strive to present an African experience and reflect a specific mode of the imagination. It is equally inaccurate to say that they have continued to treat African literature as an imitation of European literature. If there is one thing that critics have been aware of, it is the autonomy of African literature, and their use of the so-called Western criteria in its evaluation does not by any means imply that African literature is an offshoot of Western literature. One would very much like to know on what evidence Mrs James has come to the remarkable conclusion that such criticism makes African literature foreign to the African. It is not enough to throw statements glibly around; one must try to demonstrate them.

Turning from the enunciation of the critic's duties to a consideration of

* Mrs James's review appears on p. 149 (Ed.).

the book itself, she suggests that I have nothing to add to the analysis of Achebe's novels after the 'competent' work done by Irele and Killam. Where I attempt to be original, as in my discussions of Unoka and Okonkwo's society, my propositions, she claims, are 'risible'. May I stress that I am not an historian or social anthropologist writing about life in nineteenth-century Iboland, but a literary critic looking carefully at what is *present* in the novel; in this process I see that Okonkwo's society is a highly competitive and acquisitive one. It should be obvious that this is what I mean by 'rat-race'. Mrs James should also surely realise that Unoka *is* out of place in his society. It may well be that the artist in traditional society has a definite role and is respected; indeed I have no doubt that Okonye, the other musician, is cast in this role, but I am concerned not with the artist's role in traditional society, but with Achebe's *presentation* of a particular artist, and I am sure that Unoka is presented as an outcast. In fact I state quite clearly the kind of artist he is, by comparing him to beatniks and bohemian artists – he refuses to conform to his traditional role and is therefore ostracised, but whereas Mrs James would probably condemn him, I am sure that ultimately Achebe treats him sympathetically, carefully contrasting his more human qualities with his dehumanised son Okonkwo.

Mrs James's main point, however, is that I am completely aloof from the needs of my African reader – that of being educated as to the significance of his literature, and its application to his life. May I suggest that Mrs James reads my book again, paying particular attention to the chapters on Armah, Achebe, Okara, and Ngugi, to see whether I do not demonstrate the relevance of these novels to the contemporary African situation? Mrs James rests her case mainly on two quotations from the book, but she fails to demonstrate clearly how the first shows my aloofness from the needs of my African reader. Is it that she disagrees with my view that the novelist is free to choose whatever theme he wishes, provided he keeps within the bounds of human endeavour? If this is the case, then it flagrantly contradicts her subsequent remark that it is not the writer's subject alone which argues the significance and success of the work. Surely, this is the point that I am also making in the Laye passage. Or is she suggesting that Camara Laye, and all African novelists for that matter, must deal with the anti-colonial struggle? This is surely a dangerous and arrogant doctrine. If Mrs James had written in a calmer, less vehement frame of mind, she would probably have seen the illogicalities and contradictions in her article. On the second quotation, I can only say that it is perverse to deduce from my statement that I feel there is something inherently wrong with cultural and sociological matters as the themes of novels. Mrs James herself realises later that I have nothing but praise for Achebe's *Things*

Fall Apart and Amadi's *The Concubine*; this alone should have drawn her attention to the illogicality of her earlier remark. I was merely suggesting that the sociological theme has been overworked.

Mrs James allows her prejudices to betray her into making the most sweeping generalisations, such as that my views originate entirely from my western education rather than from my being conversant with the needs of the African public. This kind of woolly talk about the needs of the majority of the African public always suggests to me that ideological considerations are coming to the fore, with possibly disastrous consequences. Without launching into historical, political, or sociological disquisitions, I make a strenuous attempt in my book to demonstrate the novelists' awareness of the forces at work in their society, and to discuss these forces as they are presented in the novels, without distorting the novelists' viewpoints. I don't know that within the context of the book itself it is legitimate to do more in order to relate these novels to their cultural and sociological background. But Mrs James accuses me of eschewing sociological criticism. That this is a distortion will be clear to anyone who reads my chapters on Achebe, Amadi, Armah, Okara, and Ngugi with the slightest degree of attention and fair-mindedness. Since I am not giving historical or sociological lectures, I do not see that my task should go beyond the interpretation of the society *presented* in the novels. In fact, the quotation she cites from my book to prove her point, ought to have demonstrated to her that I am concerned both with what the novelist is saying about his society and the way in which he says it. It is therefore inaccurate to talk about my being interested in formal criticism alone.

Mrs James takes me further to task for making 'innumerable references' only to European literature. I would have thought that in a book on African literature it is surely legitimate to refer for comparative purposes to non-African literature, and it should be obvious that in the circumstances the only non-African literature I could refer to was Western literature. But it seems that Mrs James's real quarrel with me is not that I refer to European literature alone, but that I should have referred to it at all, since such works are of little value to the African reader who reads less and less English (or European?) literature. One wonders whether this startling declaration is a statement of fact based on evidence, or wishful thinking. Since she is so interested in the educational needs of her students, perhaps one ought to stress that it is part of the academic's task to handle the spirit of inquiry and curiosity in his or her students and to stimulate them into reading works they would otherwise not read. A comparative study of European works and African literature will greatly enrich the understanding and enjoyment of both, and will most probably enable Mrs

James to overcome her students' inability or reluctance to respond to Western literature.

Mrs James then goes on to make a series of highly questionable statements. There is, she says, a total system of world truth, but there is, apparently, a different system of truth for the African; the African critic must take into account the fact that the African peoples are the most oppressed and dehumanised in the world. This may well be true, but what has it got to do with the criticism of works like *The Radiance of the King*, *The Concubine* or *The African Child*? According to her, the African critic, like the African writer, must be committed and subjective. This is the enunciation of a critical doctrine which I find both dangerous and irresponsible, and which totally disregards the educational needs of readers. I will never accept that the critic should allow his commitment to influence his criticism. On the contrary, I will maintain that the African critic, like other critics, has to strive to be as objective as possible, or his criticism will be valueless. He must approach the work in question with an open mind, honestly prepared to evaluate and illuminate what he finds there. It is dangerous for any critic to try to read his ideological prejudices and preconceptions into a work.

As an example of my lack of commitment and 'consciousness' Mrs James cites my use of the word 'natives' which she claims, is unpolitical. It seems to me that only those who are preoccupied with ideological matters will question the use of the word in reference to the true people of Kenya as opposed to the white invaders. It is equally unpolitical, she claims, to suggest that *A Grain of Wheat* recalls Conrad's *Lord Jim*; and she proceeds to ask with astonishing naiveté: 'Must the African always copy from his white masters? Can he not be credited with a certain amount of originality?' Who said anything about white masters? The reviewer's most illogical question does not follow from my statement. It is a rhetorical device to switch the argument to another plane; it is an irrational attempt to appeal to the emotions and nationalistic feelings of African readers, rather than to their reason; it is a device commonly used, as a last resort, by those incapable of rational argument, and I would not have expected it from someone of Mrs James's intelligence and sensibility. Her own reading of my book should have told her that I reserve the warmest commendations for *A Grain of Wheat*.

Shifting her ground once more, however, she makes the even more startling statement that such comparisons are fruitless since the African student is not likely to have read the work in question. She must surely be a splendid academic; not only will she give her students what they want to read, she will not mention anything that they are not likely to have read. She shifts her ground again, questioning the basis of my comparison, since the similarity between the two novels is only a loose one. Here she (I hope accidentally) misquotes me. My exact words were: 'Its complexity of form recalls the involutions of Conrad's *Lord Jim* on which it seems consciously to have been modelled.' My comparison of the two works relates to their form only, not to their subject matter.

Even assuming that Irele has finally mapped the course that African criticism should follow, the verdict on Mrs James's pontifical accusation that I have done nothing to further the development of African criticism along these lines, must surely be at best 'not proven'. I suspect, however, that her real quarrel with me is that by the application of my criteria, certain novels which she values because of their preoccupation with sociological and cultural matters are shown to be mediocre. When she says that the African critic should be subjective and committed and should look at African literature from a definite historical reality, I suspect that all she requires from these novels is that they should deal with cultural, social, and political problems, and that they should concern themselves with the dehumanisation and oppression of the African peoples; the quality of the novelist's execution should not matter to the subjective, committed critic.

My critical position is quite different. I certainly feel the novelist must deal with the burning issues of his society, and the critic should concern himself with the novelist's treatment of these issues, whether social, cultural, political, or religious, and should show how relevant these novels are to the contemporary situation; but he should also evaluate the novelist's art. I certainly do not feel we must commend writers merely for their presentation of the oppression and dehumanisation of the African people, if their art is defective.

On the Business of Literary Criticism
With special reference to Bahadur Tejani's article: 'Can the Prisoner Make a Poet?'[1]

M. J. Salt

It is my contention, in this article, that Mr Tejani's preconceived ideas and opinions about South Africa, and about Dennis Brutus, have gravely distorted his 'literary criticism' of this author. I wish to maintain – without making any extravagant claims for Brutus as a poet – that he does deserve serious critical attention. Before I can safely start on this central part of the paper, however, I must mention one important problem that will confront the reader of Mr Tejani's essay. It is, I suggest, sometimes very difficult to understand what he is saying.

I would like to begin, then, with the tentative remark that it is partly the business of literary criticism to make 'sense' of literature – to interpret it. In this respect, the critic has a certain duty to his author and to his reading public, and this duty cannot be taken lightly. Mr Tejani's prose, however, is sometimes a little less than meaningful:

> The publishers having gone all the way with Brutus's wavering mind have created a waywardness for themselves which is rare. (p. 132)

and:

> The poet and the publishers, their assumption of men and the reading public, will no doubt serve as an open warning to our understanding of South Africa for a while to come. (p. 143)

This unpalatable fact could well condition, of course, my own interpretation of Tejani's paper. My quotations strongly suggest, I think, that at certain points in this paper one simply can't be sure what this critic is talking about. This is not a valuable quality in a critical essay.

128

The central preoccupation of my paper must now be stated. I would like to examine the ways in which Mr Tejani's preconceived ideas and opinions about South Africa, and about Dennis Brutus, have affected his literary criticism of this author. (The basic problem, here, is not a new one: we might cite the case of the convinced atheist who wishes to explicate, or interpret, the works of Dante.) We might profitably begin our discussion of this problem by noting two statements which Tejani makes about South Africa and the white South Africans: statements which appear in the very first part of his paper:

To the mind of the East African the white South African is a bizarre inhuman phenomenon. (p. 130)

and:

Quite understandably, not until the deeper shades of suspicion have been removed by long personal contact can we believe in anything that is said by a white South African, or view anyone who toes the line of non-resistance without natural hostility. (p. 130)

I believe that in some parts of his paper, Tejani assumes that Brutus does have a certain 'sympathy' for the white racists, and I also think that he assumes that Brutus does toe 'the line of non-resistance' in some of his poems. The point of view outlined in my quotations may indeed be quite 'understandable', even if the gross generalisations involved render it, in another – and more academic – sense, less than 'acceptable'. Certainly, we can be in no doubt as to Tejani's point of view on this matter. He goes on to define his attitude to Dennis Brutus in a later part of his paper:

For him no reserves of energy, no courage of beliefs from deep within, no conflict, no fortitude to buoy him against the hostile environment.
(p. 134)

and:

Finally, if it is thought that every writer's pen is bound to suffer in comparison with another's, let me point to the fact emerging out of his poetry that weakens the foundation of Brutus's verse. The poet's special designation 'coloured' has important implication in the South African situation. By such an intermediary arrangement, a man may belong in his own mind, to two races at once – 'black' and 'white', or to neither. But never to the third one, the 'human' race, that which is his own. In case this point is thought nebulous, the reader should refer to Ezekiel Mphahlele's story 'A Point of Identity' where according

129

to this recognized writer on the South African question, the life-springs of Karel Almeida, the hero of the story, go slack when he opts for 'coloured' instead of 'black' identity. The choice, partly enforced and partly self-orientated, takes him away from human brotherhood.

(p. 139)

We can hardly accept the first of these two statements, as it stands, because up to that point Tejani had only quoted a few lines of Brutus's poetry. (He had, it is true, given the titles of a number of other poems.) The statement will quite properly remain an inference, then, until such time as it is backed up with supporting references. I might say, in passing, that the critic's reference to poem no. 16 cannot support his opinion. The second quotation would seem to indicate that Brutus himself is divorced from the 'human brotherhood' – whatever that means – unless he opts for a specifically 'black', or a specifically 'white', identity. This statement, which again involves the use of vague generalisation, might well strike us as being rather nonsensical. However that might be, Tejani goes on to say that 'Brutus's strength in dealing with experience is uncertain',[2] and he further suggests that:

> Brutus, like Almeida, is not free from the cruel irony imposed by his racist government. He is unable to choose between the 'human' truths, of justice and freedom, and the 'racial' truths, which are continuous comparison and equivocation based on class and culture. There is besides a sense of underlying religiousness in his poetry which makes him suspect. Indeed the simplicity and earnestness of tone *is* religious. Whereas elsewhere this may be a positive or neutral quality, it is purely negative in South Africa – of the seventies. There is no greater deterrent to protest against outrageous tyranny than a religion of love. (p. 140)

Once again, the quotation ends with a gross generalisation. One of Tejani's points seems to be that a religion of love is enshrined within Brutus's poetry, and that one manifestation of this – and of the poet's supposed failure to choose between 'human' and 'racial' truths – is a certain sympathy for the white South Africans. It also seems to be implied that this 'religion of love' has led the poet to 'toe the line of non-resistance'. As an instance of this sort of thinking, Tejani suggests that in the poem 'The Mob':

> . . . the poet's refrain, 'O my people' gives his heart to them. (p. 140)
> (i.e. to the white South Africans.)
> (The parenthesis is mine.)

This might well be what Mr Tejani wants to believe, but does a reading of the poem justify his assumption? With proper reference to the poem,

130

we might consider whether Mr Tejani's hostile attitude towards Dennis Brutus has helped him to 'appreciate' – in the fullest sense of that word – Brutus's poetry.

I must begin my inquiry into this matter by giving the full context for the quotation, cited above. After recording the last six lines of the poem, the critic says:

> It is legitimate to ask who are the poet's people and if they deserve his sympathy. The mob that attacked those who struggle for the minimal freedom in South Africa are literally faceless, faithless, and, as Dostoevsky said, without the gift of human tears. Yet the poet's refrain, 'O my people' gives heart to them. (p. 140)

Tejani seems to believe, then, that far from actually criticising the white racists, Brutus has given 'his heart to them'. He describes these white South Africans as being 'faceless' people, taking his cue, no doubt, from Brutus himself:[3]

> These are the faceless horrors
> that people my nightmares
> from whom I turn to wakefulness
> for comforting, ... (p. 36)

These lines, which are not quoted by Mr Tejani, do not seem to indicate that Brutus's opinion of the white racists is very different from Mr Tejani's opinion of them. The poet is saying, in effect, that these particular white South Africans resemble – in some ways at least – the grotesque figures and creatures that 'people' his nightmares. But, says Brutus, at least one can escape from one's nightmares by simply waking up. The trouble is that to wake up and see the white protestors attacking the freedom fighters is not to escape from nightmares, but to be confronted with them – social nightmares. The poet sees the 'faceless horrors' attacking the protestors, and he goes on to describe them – the white South Africans who are behaving in this way – as reptiles:

> yet here I find confronting me
> the fear-blanked facelessness
> and saurian-lidded stares
> of my irrational terrors
> from whom in dreams I run. (p. 36)

We might say, for our critic's benefit, that the phrase 'saurian-lidded stares' refers to the stares of lizards and reptiles. I would suggest, therefore, that Brutus is making a strong criticism of the animalistic behaviour of the

131

white racists. His sympathies, as such, cannot be said to lie with them. They lie, by implication, with the very people who are being attacked by these 'monsters'. We must be careful, then, over our interpretation of the line 'O my people'. I would like to make it clear that I don't think that Brutus ever makes Tejani's fundamental distinction between those South Africans who are 'inhuman' and those who are 'human'. As far as I can see, the poet regards all South Africans – regardless of their colour or creed – as basically, and importantly, human beings. It is just that some of them – here the white racists – are acting as though they were animals. The line 'O my people', then, refers to the white South Africans in the poem, who are as much the poet's 'people' – in the sense that I have been insisting upon – as the black South Africans. The poem makes it very clear, however, that it is the white racists who must somehow be made 'human' again, who must be restored to the 'human brotherhood': the brotherhood, that is, of all the other South Africans who are not racists, and who are not prejudiced. The ending of the poem challenges us: Brutus clearly states that we must face the racists with criticism and that we must struggle to 'educate' and rehabilitate them:

> O my people
> what have you done
> and where shall I find comforting
> to smooth awake your mask of fear
> restore your face, your faith, feeling, tears. (p. 36)

The strong implication is, I think, that it will be impossible for one man to accomplish this task. We must all be directly involved in the struggle. (The fact that Brutus seems to envisage this struggle as a non-violent one seems to worry Mr Tejani. I would suggest that, on this matter, we cannot dictate terms to the poet. To do so would be to introduce our own pre-conceived ideas about the nature of revolutionary struggle. In the light of such 'independence' struggles as that waged by the Indian people, one can surely accept Dennis Brutus's point of view without necessarily agreeing with it. It is certainly the case, I think, that Brutus argues his position with an honest conviction. His thoughts on the nature of revolutionary struggle often seem to resemble those of such leaders as Dr Martin Luther King. If one doesn't accept that Brutus has the right to a point of view on this matter, then one's criticism of nearly all his 'prison' poems must be prefaced with some sort of disclaimer of Brutus *the man*.) The real point is that we are now in a position to see that Mr Tejani has simply misinterpreted this poem. We can hardly say, as he does, that Brutus has given his heart to them – these white racists, these reptile-humans. To make such a comment is surely to misunderstand this poem. Tejani may want to believe that Brutus is siding with the whites, but we have seen that this is surely not the case.

I would like to look next at Tejani's analysis of the poem 'Their Behaviour'. Once again, it is my contention that the critic's preconceived ideas about Brutus have seriously distorted his interpretation of this particular poem. *A propos* of this work, Tejani states that:

> Brutus even believes that when the white South Africans celebrate Blood River Day on 16 December:
> Their guilt
> is not so very different from ours. (p. 140)

He goes on to suggest that:

> . . . according to Brutus the only difference between 'white South African guilt' and others, in the poem on page 26, is that the former is:
> 'On a social, massive organized scale
> which magnifies enormously.'
> I find it difficult to accept this judgement based on size and numbers. His interpretation of guilt itself is questionable. Considering the attempted genocide on both sides in the 1830s, the history of such a situation is necessarily complex. Brutus's interpretation is not. He has chosen the 'safe' way of contrasting individual guilt complex based on misuse of personal power, greed, and instinctive temptation.
> (pp. 140–1)

(It is a feature of this article that when Mr Tejani cites Brutus he often misquotes him. Eleven of his quotations are marred in this way. There are four errors in the lines that are cited above. It is hardly satisfactory that this should be so.) The critic rightly complains, here, of the need to feel a quantitative, and qualitative difference between our 'personal' guilt and the guilt of the racists, and their racist regime. I fancy, however, that he has not realised that Brutus is making just this sort of distinction in his poem 'Their Behaviour'. Brutus begins this particular poem by remarking upon a specific, observable trait of human nature – man's obvious joy in the 'arbitrary exercise of power'. This attitude of mind is by no means restricted to people of any one colour or creed. But, to recognise that we do sometimes act in this way is a necessary preliminary to the regeneration of our more 'social', and more 'human' instincts and feelings. The white South African racists do not entertain such thoughts of 'regeneration'. Instead, they seek to stimulate their anti-social, and anti-human, instincts and feelings:

> so, in their guilt,
> the bared ferocity of teeth,

chest-thumping challenge and defiance,
the deafening clamour of their prayers
to a deity made in the image of their prejudice . . . (p. 28)

and, from the poem on page 26:

> Each year on this day
> they drum the earth with their boots
> and growl incantations
> to evoke the smell of blood
> for which they hungrily sniff the air:
>
> guilt
> drives them to the lair
> of primitiveness
> and ferocity:

The white racists do sense their 'guilt' – a guilt born of their long years of domination and tyranny – but they seek to sublimate it by giving further expression to the grossest forms of 'animalistic behaviour'. In the two poems that I have quoted, the whites are characterised as 'gorillas' and 'savage beasts'. The strong rhythms in these lines – the 'pointing' of the adjectives and nouns which have pejorative connotations – convey this sense of an outpouring of bitter, and bestial, emotions. (They also register the poet's sense of outrage at this state of affairs.) By way of contrast, the first part of 'Their Behaviour' depicts a far more rational process: a man's sensitive examination of his own soul. These two sections of 'Their Behaviour', then, are forcibly juxtaposed:

> Their guilt
> is not so very different from ours:
> —who has not joyed in the arbitrary exercise of power
> or grasped for himself what might have been another's
> and who has not used superior force in the moment when he could,
> (and who of us has not been tempted to these things?)   (p. 28)

We might say, I think, that moral regeneration is more likely to spring from this sensitive examination of the soul. The racists, on the other hand, debase their own humanity and, in the process, they oppress and seek to debase others:

> and our men
> are bloated with bloody thoughts; inflated sacrifices
> and grim despairing dyings.

This quotation comes from the poem on page 27, but it is linked thematically to the last section of 'Their Behaviour'. There, we see that the racists are not prepared merely to 'glory' in their bestial instincts: they seek to create a political state which will manifest these instincts 'on a social, massive, organised scale/ which magnifies enormously'.[4] It will now be clear, I think, that there is both a quantitative and qualitative difference between 'their' guilt, and 'ours'. We must reject Tejani's assertion that:

> He has chosen the 'safe' way of contrasting individual guilt complex based on misuse of personal power, greed, and instinctive temptation.
>
> (p. 141)

Brutus has not merely chosen a 'safe' way of reflecting on the significance of this occasion. He has, instead, criticised the bestiality of the white racists, and indicated the viciousness of their prejudice. At the same time, he has made it clear that prejudice and anti-social feelings can sometimes hold sway in our minds too. Unless we recognise this fact, he seems to say, we cannot hope to be in a position to control these feelings when they come to the fore. Brutus has also commented – by implication – upon the plight of those who are ruled by these 'human-reptiles'. We might also suggest that he has described some of the motives which inspired – if that is the right word – the whites on that first Blood River Day. I am not sure, then, that we can agree with our critic when he says that he understands what 'the poet has in mind'.[5]

As a further example of the operation of preconceived ideas and opinions upon Mr Tejani's criticism, I would like to cite his remarks on the poem which begins 'Presumably/one should pity'.[6] They deserve, in fact, to be quoted in full:

> In an untitled poem, the latter [Brutus] comes so close to the doctrine of the other cheek that hardly anything positive may remain:
>
> 'But it is best to shutter the mind
>   and heart
> eyes, mouth and spirit;
> say nothing feel nothing and do not let
>   them know
> that they have cause for shame.'

'Them' and 'They' are relative here and it is uncertain in the whole poem what the pronouns refer to. Even the 'old fighters' to which the pronouns seem to be connected, do not have any explicit sense. But the creed of submission and withdrawal that the poet expounds is very disturbing. (p. 142)

Suffice it to say, I think, that Brutus is not in any way expounding the 'creed of submission and withdrawal'. Tejani might like to think that he is, but does the poem back up his opinion? The poem begins by saying, quite unambiguously, that 'Presumably/ one should pity the frightened ones/ the old fighters . . .'.[7] We might conclude, I think, that within the context of the book *Letters to Martha* these old fighters are almost bound to be 'freedom fighters'. Brutus notices that they have given up the struggle – 'the old fighters/ who now shrink from contact:' – but he refuses to condemn them, or judge them. He is not being perverse here, but merely recognising the obvious fact that human motivation is often a complex thing, and hidden from our understanding. But he goes on to say – again quite unambiguously – that their giving up of this social struggle is a 'cause for shame'. That is to say, he criticises these men for not struggling. We come then to the strange conclusion that what Mr Tejani would have liked Brutus to say, and what he did say, are one and the same thing. (I am assuming that Tejani wanted the poet to criticise these back-sliders, and to encourage further 'struggle' for the future.)

At the risk of boring the reader, I would now like to suggest that Tejani's own point of view – as outlined a little earlier in this paper – has obstructed his judgement of another poem: the poem which is headed 'For Canon L. John Collins'. This section of the critic's paper starts with the following quotation:

> Temperamentally Brutus is unsuitable to take on the sophisticated might of the South African Government. This unsuitability leads to simplistic conclusions of hope without struggle. (p. 142)

These remarks are – as we have come to expect – gross generalisations. They do not square with what we have so far seen of Brutus's philosophy of 'struggle', and they do not square with the thoughts that Brutus expresses in his poem 'For Daantje – on a New Coin envelope'. Since this particular poem so clearly expresses the poet's point of view on this matter, I would like to quote the following lines from it:

> And I, who cannot stir beyond these walls,
> who shrink the temptation of any open door
> find hope in thinking that repose
> can be *wrung* from these iron-hard rigidities. (p. 30)

The word that I have italicised does, I think, convey the strong impression that we will have to struggle to achieve 'repose'. Now, *a propos* of the work cited above, Mr Tejani wants to suggest that:

In two poems written on the day he left South Africa for the free world, there are revelations which show the poet pushing back the edge of experience for illusions. In 'To Canon Collins' he argues that Man's scientific prowess, his mastery over time and space, denotes a positive note, so that:

> 'Pain shall be quiet, the prisoned free and
> wisdom sculpt justice from the world's
> jagged mass.' (p. 142)

(I should like to point out that the errors in this quotation are not mine.) Still, I am reasonably sure that the critic would say that here again we have the assertion of 'hope without struggle' – of an 'illusion'. But, it seems to me that much of what Brutus is saying, in this poem, is ironical. In order to demonstrate this point, I shall have to quote the whole of the second section of this poem:

> now that all canons of space-time are dumb
> and obey the assertions of resolute will
> and an intricate wisdom is machined to leash
> ten thousand horses in world-girdling flight,
> how shall we question that further power
> waits for a leap across gulfs of storm; (p. 34)

The basic point seems to be that man has had to struggle to achieve his technological revolution. He has developed an 'intricate wisdom', and applied this wisdom – 'machined' it, if you like – to produce his technology. A number of words in the poem describe the awesome power of these machines – for instance their ability to make possible 'world-girdling' flight. Now, the last two lines that I have quoted above strongly suggest that a further huge effort – of both body and mind – will be needed to make possible a 'leap across gulfs of storm'. This last image obviously refers to the strife that exists between men, and in this context it must especially refer to the racial 'storms' in South Africa. The irony is, it seems to me, that while men are prepared to effect a 'technological revolution' and to work for it, they are less prepared to struggle to establish a 'social revolution' – a revolution that will grant an equality of opportunity to all men. Brutus indicates that this last revolution will require a massive effort; as much effort, in fact, as we have put into our struggle against the elements, and the hostile environment. He doesn't even leave this matter in doubt – except of course to Mr Tejani. 'Justice', after all, must be sculpted – cut, or chipped or hammered – 'from the world's/ jagged mass'.[8]

We might show, I think, that in any number of cases Mr Tejani's

137

preconceptions about Dennis Brutus have seriously interfered with his understanding of the poems, and with his 'literary criticism'. His response to the 'eighteenth letter' will be my last example. Tejani's first comment about this poem is, to say the least, rather unbecoming:

> The eighteenth letter seems to me quite contrived and in the main doubtful. (p. 137)

What are we, the readers, to make of that? As it stands, it is such a vague statement! (It seriously disturbs that the paper is so full of this kind of writing.) Still, we won't be in a position to assess the validity of the statement until we have quoted it in full, and in the proper context. This is as follows:

> The eighteenth letter seems to me quite contrived and in the main doubtful. There is an uneasy lack of seriousness which disturbs, which renders the confrontation between the prisoner and machine-gunning sentry melodramatic:
>
> > 'I scampered to the window
> > and saw splashes of light
> > where the stars flowered.'
>
> Throughout the whole poem, the line that disturbs most is 'scampering to the window'. Can Nature be surveyed, responded to, and made the most of in such a hurry? In prison where time itself stands still? What does one glean from such an experience either about the poet or his environment? The sentry's barked warning to the prisoner when he plunged the cell into darkness to 'see' the stars, is as natural a reaction to such momentary foolhardiness, as our doubt of the poet's relationship to Nature. (p. 137)

Tejani might well ask 'What does one glean from such an experience either about the poet or his environment?' The sheer naivety of these earnest questions – 'Can Nature be surveyed, responded to, and made the most of in such a hurry?' – surprises, and I must say, offends. Hasn't this man read Soyinka, or Clark, or Wordsworth? We do not expect such foolishness in our literary criticism. However, this foolishness can only be demonstrated by an analysis of the poem.

I suggest that a reading of the poem indicates that it is entirely serious – every line of it. The prisoner's first thought was to 'try and find the stars'. These seem to be not so much stars of fortune as images of a man's natural freedoms – his right to independence, his right to dream and to create fantasy worlds, and his right to be creative. They seem to signify, amongst other things, life, beauty, and hope. They also seem to stand guardians of

138

the world 'outside' – a world denied to the prisoners. These men are, indeed, the inmates of a purely artificial environment:

> And through the haze
> the battens of fluorescents made
> I saw pinpricks of white
> I thought were stars. (p. 19)

The inhumanity of prison life seems to engender a pathetic passivity in the convicts, a passivity bred of boredom and hopeless frustration. Action – any action – becomes nothing less than a hazardous adventure:

> Greatly daring
> I thrust my arm through the bars
> and easing the switch in the corridor
> plunged my cell in darkness. (p. 19)

It is, indeed, an irony of prison life that the everyday activities, which we take so much for granted, are there invested with the utmost importance and significance. It is another irony that a prisoner, who is already so cut off from the world, should have to plunge his cell into darkness to find privacy. For a fleeting moment, then, Brutus escapes into himself, into his own private world – the world of Brutus the poet, and Brutus the man:

> I scampered to the window
> and saw splashes of light
> where the stars flowered. (p. 19)

It is this sense of liberation, this momentary throwing off of the terrible yoke of servitude, which validates the use, here, of the word 'scampering'. When Mr Tejani attempts to pass off this action as mere 'foolhardiness', he does no little disservice to both the poem and the poet. (It is surely one of the many inconsistencies in this paper, that our critic appears to censure Brutus for struggling against the prison system. Presumably, in this poem, the poet shouldn't 'hope' and shouldn't 'struggle': he should be passive.) I do not doubt, for a moment, that some will detect a comic irony in these lines. The significance allotted to one small event might seem to dictate this. But, upon reflection, the comic irony will be seen to serve the more serious effects of the whole poem. Whichever way we approach the lines, we must notice the way in which the rhythms change, and are the servants to the 'sense'. Suspense gives way to excitement, and this in turn makes way for a moment of recognition and a moment of fulfilment, as 'the stars flowered'. The only 'foolhardiness', here, is in the prisoner's actually wanting to defy authority – in his actually thinking this to be possible, in his wanting to be different, to be himself. Did he really think that he had a right to such freedoms? Did he really think that the prison authorities, and thereby the state, would agree to such a thing? (We might also mention, in passing, that the use of the word 'scampering' evokes memories of childhood experiences – those experiences which are born of freedom.) The prison guards, of course, will have none of this. Their concern is to 'incarcerate' the spirit of a man, as well as his body:

> But through my delight
> thudded the anxious boots
> and a warning barked
> from the machine-gun post
> on the catwalk. (p. 19)

The use of the word 'through', here, indicates the validity of my preceding remarks. The convict's whole experience – an experience of the body and soul – is pierced and deflated. The guards are anxious about the prisoner, then, for the wrong reasons and their denial makes them seem less than human when they 'bark' their commands and orders to the man. We might also say, I suggest, that at this point the prison system stands as an image for the political system operating in South Africa: a system which denies men their basic right of freedom. The ending of the poem is itself ironical. It invites us to ponder why it is that:

> . . . it is the brusque inquiry
> and threat
> that I remember of that night
> rather than the stars. (p. 19)

This inquiry will, I suggest, lead us to discover a great deal about the prisoner, the prisoner's way of life, his society, and what we might venture to call 'human nature'.

The basic point, then, is that the critic's own point of view has prevented him from obtaining any clear understanding of the poetry of Dennis Brutus. It seems to be clear, I suggest, that when a critic is not prepared to take his author seriously, when he is not even prepared to view him as a 'man' – as a fellow human being who is entitled to a certain sympathy, and a certain understanding – it is surely best to forgo any attempt to criticise his work. It is a pity that this is so, in this case. Mr Tejani is certainly right when he argues that we must ask 'fundamental' critical questions about Brutus's poetry. (Questions about the language that the poet uses, about the 'form' of his poems, about the integrity of some of his prose-poetry and about the uneven standard of his work.) The trouble is that this critic asks the wrong questions: questions which are formulated on the basis of strong preconceptions and opinions about Brutus. It is the intrusion of these 'opinions' into his literary criticism that finally invalidates much of Mr Tejani's paper on the poetry of Dennis Brutus.

NOTES

1. Bahadur Tejani, 'Can the Prisoner Make a Poet? A Critical Discussion of *Letters to Martha*, by Dennis Brutus', in *African Literature Today*, No. 6, ed. Eldred D. Jones (London, Heinemann, 1973).
2. ibid., p. 135.
3. Dennis Brutus, *Letters to Martha* (London, Heinemann, 1969).
4. ibid., p. 28.
5. Tejani, op. cit., p. 141.
6. Brutus, op. cit., p. 24.
7. loc. cit.
8. ibid., p. 34.

REVIEWS

Charles R. Larson
The Emergence of African Literature

Solomon Ogbede Iyasere

Charles R. Larson, *The Emergence of African Literature*, Indiana University Press, 1972.

Since African literature has become a recognised field of literary study in institutions of higher learning, both African and non-African belletristic critics have objected to the Eurocentric and socio-anthropological approaches usually taken in the criticism of African fiction. As several critics have pointed out, and as I have argued elsewhere,[1] the 'content-oriented' approach insisted upon by the anthropologists, self-styled Africanists, and erratic Western reviewers, is unqualifiably inadequate. Significantly, their equation of traditionalism (the ethnic reportage of ancient, exotic customs) with literary merit, has often led to the debasement of this literature, and made readers come to view African literature less as art than as a socio-anthropological document. Concomitantly, several other critics have also pointed out that the Eurocentric approach – the application of Western aesthetics concepts to African literature, has led to a distortion and dehydration of this literature. In their view the 'culture-oriented' approach based upon some concept of 'African aesthetics' is more relevant and more vital to the criticism of the literature. Yet no critic, until Charles Larson's *The Emergence of African Fiction* appeared, has, with any consistency, attempted to define what this 'African aesthetics' is, or to defend, on literary grounds, those curious aspects of African fiction, such as lack of character delineation, undisciplined plot, the high frequency of didactic endings, or, better still, those oddities that permeate works such as Amos Tutuola's – elements which perplex Western sensibilities.

In Chapter I of *The Emergence of African Fiction*, the most insightful chapter, I might hasten to add, Larson, in demonstrating the uniqueness and vitality of African contemporary literature, stresses the influences of the oral tradition – influences which most critics have ignored. Speci-

143

fically, he deals with how the contemporary African writers have employed their inherited oral rhetorical narrative devices as artistic techniques to explore, define, and shape their vision of the socio-historical realities into significant, artistic wholes; and, more importantly, as the means of reshaping the conventional novel form. With sufficient documentation and clarity, Larson goes on to re-emphasise how damaging and inadequate the Eurocentric and anthropologically oriented approaches to African literature have been. Underlining the fact that African literature be considered art, not some cultural trove, Larson then sets forth a more 'objective' working hypothesis upon which the Western and non-Western critics should base their evaluations of African literature. First of all, Larson singles out the fact 'that the African novel is frequently different from its Western counterpart and that the differences can be attributed to cultural background', and, secondly, 'that in spite of several typical unities which are generally considered to hold the Western novel together, that is, to give it its structural background, the African writer has created new unities which give his fiction form and pattern'. With this bipartite hypothesis established, Larson proceeds in the following chapters to examine the works of the first and second generation anglophone African novelists, starting with the 'archetypal' model provided by Chinua Achebe's *Things Fall Apart* (Nigeria) and concluding with the experimental and forward-looking works of Wole Soyinka (Nigeria) and Ayi Kwei Armah (Ghana). The intervening chapters deal respectively with Onitsha market literature of Nigeria (chapter 3); the Tutuolan world (chapter 4); the 'situational novel': works of James Ngugi from Kenya (chapter 5); characters and modes of characterisation: Chinua Achebe, James Ngugi, and Peter Abrahams from South Africa; assimilated négritude: Camara Laye's *Le regard du roi* and, lastly, the West African gothic of Lenrie Peters' *The Second Round*.

Larson's definition of the hypotheses with which African fiction can be judiciously evaluated is an impressive one. Yet, one cannot but point out the flagrant limitations of Larson's criteria. First of all, they are too vague, too general to be sufficiently precise and useful to a discussion of the corpus of African literature. Secondly, the works to which Larson applies his standards are too few, too convenient, and too selective to demonstrate the vitality and validity of the criteria. Moreover, the tracking down of oral influences in African fiction as Larson's approach demands, encourages eclecticism and may become an end in itself. And often this hunt for remnants of the oral tradition entails an excusing and obscuring of elements which, though effective in an oral work, are not so appropriate in a written piece: that a feature is a vestige of the oral tradition does not necessarily make it good. More of this later. In all, a crucial point Larson seems to miss is that criticism depends far less on theoretical systems or codified hypotheses than on the quality of the critic's mind – his intelligence and learning, his critical sensitivity and judgement. Good criticism is not an end in itself, but a means to the greater understanding and appreciation of a literary work.

But the real test of any hypothesis or critical criteria comes, of course, in the application of that hypothesis and of those criteria to a specific matter of elucidating a particular text. And here, in the application of Larson's theories to a discussion of the various novelists cited above, lie the most serious shortcomings of *The Emergence of African Fiction*. Typical of Larson's treatment of African fiction is his comment on the controversial ending of Chinua Achebe's *Things Fall Apart*. In his desperate defence of the ending's didactic nature and the sudden, unprepared-for shift in point of view from the detached African narrator to the erratic, egocentric District Commissioner, Larson avers, 'The shifting of point of view back and forth between an African and Western point of view symbolises the final break-up of the clan. . . . Certainly it can be argued that Achebe takes pains to make his message clear, but I feel that the shift to the District Commissioner's point of view strengthens rather than weakens the conclusion. It seems impossible for anyone to read Achebe's last chapter without being noticeably moved, and if it is didactic in the sense of tying things up too nicely, I would insist that this was Achebe's intention from the beginning and not merely an accident because of his background of oral tradition'. (*The Emergence of African Fiction*, p. 60.)

Larson's defence is too flawed to be convincing. To the increasing number of readers, the ending of *Things Fall Apart* is an unmitigated failure. Indeed Larson's own students echo the sentiments of Dr Austin J. Shelton by labelling the ending as 'overwritten, anti-climactic, and unnecessarily didactic'. Furthermore, Larson relies too heavily on the effect of the closing chapter, and ignores the fact that the emotional impact of the closing paragraphs undermines the emotional impact of the novel as a whole, as his own students are quick to point out. And Larson's insistence that the shift in point of view symbolises the final break-up of the clan is as patently absurd as David Carroll's assertion that this final scene serves to refresh our memory. Clearly there is no episode that dramatises more fully and with greater precision the final break-up of the clan than the end of Chapter XIV (*Things Fall Apart*). Lastly, unable to substantiate his argument about Achebe's intention from the text itself, Larson resorts to citing Achebe's comment on the role of the African novelist as teacher. The fallacies inherent in Larson's procedure are glaring and deal the final blow to an already weak presentation. I discuss this matter at length because the shortcomings of Larson's arguments at this point are representative in the most part of his treatment of African literature as a whole. It is as if Larson turns too quickly from critic to apologist, thus subverting his own premise that critics of African literature should not be gratuitous and patronising.

Yet to end the review of Larson's book here is to present an erroneous and one-sided position. The obvious fact is that when Larson's book is compared with such studies of African fiction as G. D. Killam's *The Novels of Chinua Achebe* (Heinemann and Africana, London and New York, 1969), Judith Gleason's *This Africa: Novels by West Africans in English and French* (Northwestern University Press, Illinois, 1965), and Margaret Laurence's *Long Drums and Cannon* (Macmillan, London, 1968), in which the critic's interest rests solely on the content to the neglect of the form, on socio-anthropological run-of-the-mill commentaries and plot summaries to the neglect of literary analysis, Larson's book appears to be a godsend. (Perhaps this is why it has received frequent praise). Occasionally, if inconsistently, Larson offers some insightful and illuminating observations on African literature in general (see his comments on the evolution of African literature, page 279) but most importantly, he treats the literature as art, a consideration African fiction has long deserved.

Although Larson's book does not deserve the extravagant accolade several critics have accorded it, a person generally interested in the study of African literature will find it useful: it offers both a general overview of African literature, and an excellent bibliography.

NOTE

1. See my forthcoming article, 'The Liberation of African Literature – A Re-evaluation of the Socio-Cultural Approach', *Books Abroad*, Summer 1974.

Eustace Palmer
An Introduction to the African Novel

Adeola James

Eustace Palmer, *An Introduction to the African Novel*, Heinemann, 1972.

In 'The Criticism of Modern African Literature',[1] Dr Abiola Irele clearly analyses the function of criticism in the development of modern African Literature. It is in the light of his profound analysis that we shall assess Dr Palmer's work, *An Introduction to the African Novel*. It is first essential to give a summary of Dr Irele's article for the benefit of those who are not familiar with it.

Modern African Literature, he says, is significant because it documents in its own historical development and in its preoccupations the tensions and the contradictions in present-day Africa. It is also a vehicle for the intensive exploration of our modern experience. African writers are groping implicitly, through the imagination, towards the creation of a new order in their societies.

Creative writing thus is playing a vital role in a modern African society. Therefore, there is a need to devise a criticism adequate to this new literature and the objectives stated above. This criticism in order to be meaningful must relate the literary expression in a clear way to the African situation and specifically to the total experience of African peoples.

Three major problems confront the critic: (i) the artistic burden placed on him owing to the fact that his writer is writing in a foreign language with incomplete mastery of the medium and its accompanying literary tradition. There is therefore a gap between the writer's means of expression and his imaginative purpose; (ii) the fact that this literature is so recent in terms of its history and is, inevitably, a hybrid thing – in Soyinka's words, 'something of a half-child'; (ii) a redirection of the modern literature for the African owing to the fact that this literature tends to be geared for a foreign audience and foreign critics.

With regard to the first problem the critic has to show how the writer

147

achieves 'a true integration of an African content with a European means of expression'. This calls for more than a superficial knowledge of both the writer's linguistic background and the borrowed medium in which the writer expresses himself.

The second problem requires the understanding of the critical function itself: 'the discrimination of values, the sharing of insights, the defence of a living culture'. The critic of modern African Literature, faced with the increasing mass of material has as his first duty to rigorously and intelligently separate 'the grain from the chaff' to ensure a healthy growth. In the process he informs us of his own personal responses based upon clear and definite criteria.

As regards the third problem, in the past the terms of reference of evaluating modern African literature have been provided by the critical tradition which has grown up alongside Western literature. The critics so far have failed to recognise the fact that although our writers use the European languages to express themselves, the most original among them do so with the conscious purpose of presenting an African experience and the best among them reflect in their works a specific mode of the imagination which derives from their African background. Critics (both foreign and African) have continued to treat modern African literature, by implication of the literary criteria adopted, as an offshoot or as an imitation of European literature thus still making African literature foreign to the African public.

The most serious task facing our critics therefore is that of relating our writers' works to the whole state and condition of our people's existence and drawing out the meaning of this literature for the African public by demonstrating not only its excellence but also its relevance.

With the above analysis in mind the reviewer started reading Dr Palmer's book with a great deal of enthusiasm for it is the first major criticism of the African novel by an African critic. One expected to find fresh ideas on the subject since he is writing from the inside. However, such expectations are unfulfilled and worst of all one is left appalled at the level of consciousness of the author.

An Introduction to the African Novel is without doubt the first closely argued critique of the African novel. The author demonstrates the relative importance of each of the novels analysed essentially from the artistic point of view. Sometimes he writes perceptively on what various novelists attempted to do. He writes better on some than others. His chapters on Ngugi are undoubtedly the best. After reading his superb interpretation of *A Grain of Wheat* the rest of the chapters seems to be on a low key because of the repetitive style.

On the whole he has nothing new to add to the analysis of Achebe's novels after the competent work already done by Irele and Killam. In fact, where he attempts to be original in his interpretation of Achebe, his propositions are often risible. For example, very few people will accept the idea of a 'rat-race' in Okonkwo's society, or that of Unoka as a dreaming artist (thus making him more out of place in his society). In respect of this latter interpretation, Palmer misconstrued the role of an artist in the traditional set-up. An artist in that society has a definite role and is respected. Unoka was not cast in this role, his dreaminess was mere escapism emanating from laziness, an attitude not to be encouraged in a society that had to fight for survival.

But these minor misreadings are not even serious charges. There are fundamental misleading judgements and misplaced emphases throughout the study arising from the writer's basic attitude to the African situation. He is completely aloof from the needs of his African reader – that of being educated as to the significance of his literature, and its application to his life. A few quotations will suffice to illustrate my point:

> Some African critics of *The African Child* deplore Laye's failure to deal with the anti-colonial struggle. One might as well condemn Jane Austen for not dealing with the French Revolution. Surely the novelist is at liberty to choose any theme within the areas of human experience. He should not be expected to deal with some political or sociological phenomenon simply because he belongs to a certain nationality, race, or tribe (p. 85).
> The decolonization of African Literature is already in progress. Novelists are becoming less preoccupied with cultural and sociological matters, and more concerned about exposing the corruption and incompetence which are so widespread in African political and governmental circles (p. 129).

One could open a parenthesis on this last quotation. In the first place the validity of the use of 'decolonisation' in this context is open to question. Secondly one might ask what is wrong with dealing with cultural and sociological matters. This leads to another dimension of the book: Palmer himself argues that both *Things Fall Apart* and *The Concubine* are among the best African novels. Yet they both deal with sociological and cultural matters. *Man of the People* is a 'decolonised' novel in the author's conception since it exposes the corruption and incompetence in African political life. But on the author's admission it is not in the same class as the other two mentioned novels. Surely it is not the subject that the writer deals with alone that argues the significance and success of that work but the life given to it as a living embodiment of the feelings of the people whom it represents.

Going back to Irele's analysis of the critical need of modern African

149

literature for which I have the utmost sympathy, Palmer's book succeeds in fulfilling the need only to a limited extent. The critic pays attention to the linguistic problem. For example, he ably demonstrates Achebe's ability to adapt his language to the exigencies of his narration using a language appropriate to the rhythm and flow of his narrative. He also points out, appropriately, the linguistic weakness in *Weep Not Child*. Conversely, he demonstrates the linguistic maturity of *A Grain of Wheat* matching the maturity of thought and deeper grasp of the problems of existence as relates to the struggle for Uhuru in Kenya. When it comes to the discrimination of values and the sharing of insights, we must be cautious in accepting Dr Palmer's views which originate entirely from his Western education rather than from his being conversant with the needs of the majority of the African public. Now when it comes to the last and most important specified requirement, that of relating African literature to its cultural background, that is where the book fails to be of any help at all.

In the first place Dr Palmer eschews sociological criticism, his basic interest being in formal criticism alone. He writes, 'one expects of a good novelist . . . that apart from his preoccupation with his message, he should have some concern for the appropriate style and show signs of technical competence' (Introduction XI).

Secondly all his innumerable references are to European literature. (*A Grain of Wheat* reminds him of *Lord Jim* and *Tristram Shandy* and Okonkwo in *Things Fall Apart* of Tess in Hardy's novel. Camara Laye's novel recalls Kafka's novels, *The Voice* recalls Eliot's *Waste Land* and Armah's novel is reminiscent of *Everyman* or Bunyan's *Pilgrim's Progress*.) These references are of little value to the African reader who reads less and less English literature. The militant ones see it as the literature of the imperialists and therefore irrelevant. Others genuinely find it difficult to empathise with the nature of the world which that literature describes and make no effort to understand it. I am not suggesting that these attitudes are necessarily correct, but this is the reality of the situation today that both the teacher and critic of African literature have to reckon with. The question is whether one cannot appreciate modern African novels fully without so much pedantic manifestations as encountered in Dr Palmer's book.

Intellectuals are entitled to demand a total system of truth about the world, but African intellectuals cannot honestly forget that the African people are the most oppressed and the most dehumanised in the world. This historical truth alone demands that our point of view be subjective, i.e. looking at African literature not from any vague or glib universal criteria (if such a thing exists) but from the definite historical reality which

150

gives birth to our literature. Hence not only the African writer but also the African critic need to be committed. 'Intellectuals or artists, thinkers or researchers, their ability is valid only if it coincides with the life of the people, if it is basically integrated into the activity, thinking and hopes of the populace.'[2] This kind of commitment is not only unfortunately lacking in Dr Palmer's work, but I doubt if his training and orientation will even allow him to agree with the basic tenet of the argument. For example, Dr Palmer sees nothing wrong with referring in his book to Kenyans as 'the natives' (see pp. 2 and 42). The least conscious person realises that 'native' is one of those words the colonialists used calculatingly to insult the African. One cannot hide behind semantic innocence. Certain words are too closely connected with our enslaved past to be thrown around carelessly without arousing certain reactions in the reader who was part of the enslavement. It is equally unpolitical to say very glibly that *A Grain of Wheat* recalls Conrad's *Lord Jim* 'on which it seems consciously to have been modelled'. Must the African always copy from his white masters? Can he not be credited with a certain amount of originality? Anyway such a derivative approach to literary criticism is as tiresome as it is fruitless. What does it mean to the average African student whom this work is supposed to benefit to say that *A Grain of Wheat* is modelled on *Lord Jim* when he is not likely to have read the novel in question? Taking the statement at its face value, similarity between these two novels is only a loose one. A personal drama of guilt and moral development which *Lord Jim* essentially is, is a far cry from a national drama at a most significant period in the people's history – a drama of pain, self questioning and groping towards a rebirth – which *A Grain of Wheat* is.

To return to my previous postulation, in demanding to know the total system of truth about the world the first step is to know the reality of our own existence disregarding any criticism of chauvinism from those who have no need to defend their being in any way. These are worthless considerations for the author. The assumption by one reviewer (see Jeremy Brooks, *Sunday Times*, 9 April 1972) that he is a European show the extent of his detachment and his complete lack of involvement which is the major cause of my quarrel with him.

In the final analysis Dr Palmer's book makes little departure from so many works of criticism by non-African critics on African literature. His point of reference is entirely that of the Western critical tradition. As such he has done nothing for the development of the criticism of modern African literature in the way that Irele has so vigorously argued for. This is an area in which so many of us feel there is still a gap.

Lastly, I would like to question the omission in this study of Oyono's and Ousmane's novels, particularly *Houseboy* and *God's Bit of Wood*.

These are two of the best and most meaningful novels in the corpus of modern African literature. It seems a grave omission in a work like this to fail to examine the pinnacle of achievement especially when the author claims he has selected 'the African novelists whose works, taken as a whole, indicate mastery of their art'.

NOTES

1. A paper read at the Ile-Ife Conference on African Writing in English, 1969.
2. Sekou Touré, 'The Political Leader Considered as the Representative of a Culture' *Présence Africaine*, xxiv–xxv, p. 119.

Eldred Durosimi Jones
The writing of Wole Soyinka

Gerald Moore
Wole Soyinka

Martin Banham

Eldred Durosimi Jones, *The Writing of Wole Soyinka*, Heinemann, 1973. Gerald Moore, *Wole Soyinka*, Evans (Modern African Writers Series), 1971.

As the publication of these two studies indicates, this seems a reasonable time to stop and take stock of Soyinka's writing, though only, I think, in terms of anticipation for what is to come. Though Soyinka remains, to an almost perverse extent, a prophet without due honour in his own country, increasing attention has been drawn to his growing stature as an important literary figure of our times by European and American critics and scholars. Professor Jones's book is the first full length study of Soyinka's plays, poetry, and novel to date, and happily comes from Africa. His dedication 'For W.S. *Our* W.S.' is not there simply for decoration!

Professor Jones was able to include the first post-detention play *Madmen and Specialists* in his consideration, and this is to be welcomed. For it seems to me that with this play (and, in conjunction with it, the revealing autobiographical work *The Man Died*, which regrettably Eldred Jones has not been able to include) Soyinka comes to both an end and a beginning. The apprenticeship is clearly over, and the fully exercised talents of the writer are now prepared for the future. The past has grown from the early pieces such as *The Trials of Brother Jero* and *The Lion and the Jewel* – witty, well-observed satires – through the deeper considerations of *The Strong Breed* and *A Dance of the Forests* to the more overtly political plays of recent years. The tone is now more despairing than before, but as brilliantly articulate as ever. Eldred Jones observes that Soyinka uses the sound of words to as much effect as he uses their meaning, and one should also add that Soyinka has a sense of theatre that makes him constantly alert to the visual image he is creating.

Both Professor Jones and Gerald Moore deal with Soyinka's first novel and his poetry as well as the plays. Both are helpful and informative about these works, though I admit to a feeling that these are not the areas where Soyinka's real strength lies, and a hope that he will concentrate his talents

153

as a poet and a narrator within his greater talent as a dramatist. Eldred Jones's book is greatly to be welcomed. For readers to whom the Yoruba background and references in Soyinka's work presents difficulties, Eldred Jones serves as an admirable and illuminating guide. While he is always alert to the practical difficulties and some of the less successful areas of Soyinka's early work, he has based his study on a most sensitive response to Soyinka's ideas and method, and upon sound scholarship. The result is a measured and perceptive comment on almost a decade-and-a-half of Soyinka's work. Gerald Moore's book was first published in 1971, and therefore misses the 'watershed' work of *Madmen and Specialists*. It is a rather more pedestrian study than Eldred Jones's, and tends to rest content with rather long accounts of the plots where the plays are concerned. It also suffers from petty irritations such as small errors of fact (Soyinka acted in *The Good Woman of Setzuan* not *The Caucasian Chalk Circle* in Ibadan, and is that really a photograph of Dapo Adelugba on page 52?) and an index that at times leads a life quite independent of the text. But if Moore's book lacks the critical liveliness of Eldred Jones's, he nevertheless offers a good introductory guide to the author. It is Moore who points to the potential of Soyinka's work in the theatre when he says:

> . . . the theatre is still the most primitive in its immediacy of all our means of organized communication. It is man speaking to men, without the interposition of canvas, microphone, camera or the printed page. Its potentialities for a society already accustomed to the ritual speech, mime and movement of the ceremonial occasion; already receptive to the transformations of personality wrought by costume, masquerade and vocal projection, would need no labouring for a young African writer eagerly making links between his distant people and his foreign, elitist education. Furthermore, drama has unique capacities for social unification, in that it works through the eye and the spoken word. Hence, if rightly shaped and performed, it can be equally accessible to literate and illiterate, to the educated Christian convert and the traditionalist, or, in Elizabethan terms, to the stagebox and the groundlings. Add the means of dissemination offered by radio and television to those already explored by the itinerant troupe, and the advantages of drama over all other literary means of expression in contemporary Africa are seen to be decisive.

It seems clear that Soyinka's example, together with that of such actor-managers as Ogunde, Ladipo and the late Ogunmola, has served to impress the truth of Moore's comments upon many in Nigeria and throughout West Africa, where we now witness a richness in theatrical material and method that should make us deeply envious. One hopes that Eldred Jones's and Gerald Moore's books will bring more attention not only to Soyinka but to the drama of Africa.

Hans M. Zell, Helene Silver *et. al.*
A Reader's Guide to African Literature

Eldred Durosimi Jones

A Reader's Guide to African Literature, compiled and edited by Hans M.
Zell and Helene Silver *et al.*, Heinemann, 1972.

A Reader's Guide to African Literature reflects in its urgency the present
bustling state of activity in African literature – pages 94 and 95 are a Stop
Press Addendum. The book will have to be constantly under this kind of
revision not only because new works and articles about them are coming
off the presses fast, but also because important articles are buried in
unlikely places. One of Soyinka's most important critical statements, 'The
Fourth Stage', in *The Morality of Art*, is not included in this very handy
guide to who's who and what's what in African literature. Inevitable
small errors should also be corrected. On p. 95, item 816, *The Gods Are
Not To Blame* is attributed in error to Obi Egbuna even though it is
correctly given to Ola Rotimi on p. 40, item 286. The volume will be the
starting point of many a thesis and term paper on African literature. This
is a bibliography, but – a remarkable thing for the genre – a readable one.
It contains snappy biographies (with photographs) of the important
writers, and brief summaries of the contents of books and important
articles. Apart from the more usual headings there are sections on Poli-
tically Committed Literature – Awolowo, Kenyatta, Nkrumah, Nyerere,
Busia, and Senghor all feature here – and on children's literature. School
teachers should be particularly grateful for this last section. Even less
usual but – judging from numerous hapless inquiries – most useful, is a
list of essential addresses of publishers and stockists of African literature.

Altogether a fine piece of work which will be an essential part of the
equipment of all critics and students of African literature.

Romanus Egudu
and Donatus Nwoga
Igbo Traditional Verse

M. J. Salt

Romanus Egudu and Donatus Nwoga, *Igbo Traditional Verse*, African Writers Series, Heinemann, 1973 (first published under the title *Poetic Heritage* by Nwankwo-Ifejika Enugu, Nigeria 1971).

There is a sense in which 'published' oral traditions lose their artistic identity. They reflect, after all, a strong sense of community life and are intimately attached to it – the traditions of the past, we might say, re-interpreted by the generations of the present. With their blend of public and more private themes, feelings, and evocations, they demand 'performance' rather than mere recitation in the study. It is in this community 'performance' that the oral traditions come so brilliantly alive.

Romanus Egudu and Donatus Nwoga, the editors and translators – one might be justified in saying the authors – of *Igbo Traditional Verse* recognise these and other problems:

> The rhythmic excitement of traditional songs can only be faintly glimpsed in the versions here. The intricate interplay between voice and drum and dance step demands a high level of expertise which, when achieved, redounds to the glory of the dance group and the excitement of the audience. (p. 5)

One of the merits of the long and helpful introduction to the book is that the authors manage to achieve a judicious balance between general state-ment and proper qualification. It is obviously the variety and complexity of the medium and the Igbo culture itself which fascinates them:

> Festivals are so many and varied in Igbo society that one need only comment on the major ones. Even what G. T. Basden regards as 'fixed festivals' differ from place to place in the society, though *Ifejoku*, that is, harvest festival, is fairly common. (p. 13)

The authors describe the major ceremonies and cultural activities of the Igbo people. Their discussion often responds to past critical and historical works on this subject. This is as it should be in a work which is addressed to 'general readers' and to 'scholars, teachers, and students of African literature' (Preface).

This intention – and the need to stimulate interest in and understanding of the oral traditions generally – necessitates both scholarly and more superficial notes to the individual poems. The contrast is between the notes appended to the poem 'Odo Masquerader Praising Himself', on page 23, and the note on page 36 which tells us that the expression 'before the sun falls' means 'Before sunset'. I hasten to add, however, that this note is not representative. Most of them will prove helpful and illuminating.

The poems themselves, even on the printed page, are often delightful and entertaining. Here, for instance, is a praise poem for a 'Beautiful Lady':

> Young lady, you are:
> A mirror that must not go out in the sun
> A child that must not be touched by dew
> One that is dressed up in hair
> A lamp with which people find their way
> Moon that shines bright
> An eagle feather worn by a husband
> A straight line drawn by God. (p. 20)

The more serious praise poems at the start of the collection can be compared to the more satirical poems in the last section. (Indeed, the book is characterised by variety of feeling, subject matter, and expression.) Personal problems – the poem 'Open the Door' on page 56 – the battle between the sexes and social problems – seen in the poem entitled 'Prostitution' on page 60 – all find a place in this last section. Other sections deal with 'Relaxation Poems', 'Dance Poems', and poems of 'Incantation' and 'Invocation'. There is, then (and we feel it very strongly), the expression of a way of life.

In a little group of verses called 'Women Against Men' we find a very dramatic little poem. It serves to remind us of the drama inherent in oral recitations of this sort. It also gives us an indication of the merits of the translation. My quotation covers about half of the printed poem:

> I was going on my way
> When the tail of my eye caught my husband
> Walking hand in hand with a girl
> I asked my husband 'What is this for?'
> He said 'Shut up, close your mouth

She is my servant'
Umu chi la edu uwa
That she was his servant
I told my mother-in-law that one of these days
The servant was going to be a wife.
The servant was going to be a wife
So that the little farm there is cut in two
The few palm trees are divided into two. (pp. 57–8)

The reader will find many such dramatic verses in this collection.

On page 41, Dr Egudu translates a poem which brings the whole collection to life. It is called 'Dance Poem: Igodo'. Here, each of the lines is punctuated with a 'humming' refrain from the chorus, and the verbal repetitions which are worked so skilfully into the verse evoke the drumming and dancing patterns which are so much a part of these composite performances.

The book, then, is a welcome addition to the Heinemann 'African Writers Series'. One can only hope that more volumes dealing with the oral traditions of Africa will soon be forthcoming.

Syl Cheyney-Coker
Concerto for an Exile

M. J. Salt

Syl Cheyney-Coker, *Concerto for an Exile*, African Writers Series, Heinemann, 1973.

Despite a fairly promising start in the '50s and early '60s, creative writing has faltered in Sierra Leone during the past decade. Poetry has been written – by students, teachers and, a small interested public – but in the main it has served to show the persistence of a pious Victorian poetic debility and, lately, a debased form of 'free verse'. Gaston Bart-Williams is an exception to this rule. He is published in a Pergamon Press Anthology (1968) and we look forward to more work from his pen. Cheney-Coker is even more of an exception. He has managed to publish a complete book of poetry and, more importantly, he has apparently dedicated his life to the pursuit of artistic excellence. Sierra Leone has thus added a poet to its small select list of dedicated artists.

Cheyney-Coker has provided us with a poetic preface to his volume *Concerto for an Exile*. He first describes his poems as 'Venomous songs!', but later qualifies this statement by saying that 'song by itself is no fertile language for death'. It is the next section of this preface which defines Cheney-Coker's attitude to and possible use of language:

> Wishing to explain my death, this terrain
> stinking of my filth
> walk on it if you dare you stand to lose
> your head!
>
> It takes the savage language of a kick
> to cure the heart of its persistent follies. . . .
> (Preface)

Personal and passionate poetry will investigate the poet's own mind: his feelings, beliefs, prejudices, and obsessions – what he calls the 'tree of agony wickedly planted in my soul'. It is a poetry which puts before us the history of the man and his society and which makes critical statements

159

about that society. The poet's weapons – evolved as shock tactics – are violent words and violent, surrealist images. We are challenged to respond and, in our turn, we the readers challenge the poet to create art; poems, as opposed to verse and mere statements.

In order to establish the main themes in this volume we have only to turn to the poem 'The Traveller' (pp. 1–2). Cheney-Coker is preoccupied with his genealogy, and the genealogy of his race. Africa was raped by the slave-traders and as if this sordid process was not enough:

> the philanthropists the beautiful assassins
> the miserable blacks wanted a new race
> despite the warnings in meteors of blazing sun. . . .(p. 1)

The image of 'mother Africa' broods beneath the surface of these poems. Her children were first driven away from the continent and then, on their return, they found no easy social solutions but only new problems:

> O my Portuguese conquistador
> do not speak to me about my genealogy
> a slaver's knife chewed my umbilical cord
> twenty-five drops of my blood Pedro da Cinta
> 1462 means nothing to me the sea to rock the belly
> was I captain of the ship William Wilberforce
> what monument shall I build to you inside
> my soul. . . . (p. 1)

The returning *asientos*, the white colonialists, the elites and the new governments of modern Africa have all, in their various ways, betrayed 'mother Africa'.

An inability to come to terms with the past conditions the poet's response to the present. Public and more private themes meet at the end of this poem. The poet meditates upon solitude:

> solitude my destiny stay solitude stay
> for tonight happiness might make love to me
> and I shall forget the tree of agony planted
> in my soul
> the tree with branches of gervas upon which my
> Argentine bird laughs! (p. 2)

There, then, are poems of bitter meditation; poems which root the anguish of the present firmly in the past; poems which examine the poet's Creole society and his own Creole identity; poems, indeed, which see in the formation of Creole society yet another 'false start' in Africa.

Cheney-Coker is at his best, as a poet, in poems like 'Toilers', 'Free-town', 'My Soul O Oasis', 'Environne', 'Agony of the Dark Child', and 'Myopia'. He is at his best, that is to say, when he rigorously controls his poetic images and uses them organically in his poems. The poem 'Environne' opens surrealistically and the surrealism is necessary in order to shock the readers out of a possible complacent attitude to the past history of Africa:

> Losing my tracks one more time
> I planted my feet deep in my heart
> I followed the laxative shadows
> emptying their bowels close to the river
> which I must cross to get to my foul ancestors. . . . (p. 21)

The poem 'Storm' deals, in part, with the conflict between the privileged and under-privileged in modern African societies. The image of the storm is established in the poem as the image of revolt. The character of the storm is evoked economically, but powerfully:

> a gathering of clouds to announce
> the coming storm the day lashes
> at the trees its giddiness of rage. . . . (p. 19)

The surrealism, in this poem, helps to define the nature of the storm:

> the day the seas flex their muscles
> like giant anacondas. . . . (p. 19)

The poem 'Toilers' depends upon a contrast between the inherent 'fruit-fulness' of Africa – especially traditional Africa – and the spiritual and physical blight which seems, to the poet, to affect most modern societies on the continent. What Cheney-Coker calls 'black opulence' rules the roost to the detriment of the poor. The title of this poem is ironical; everyone is either toiling for nothing or for the wrong things.

All of these poems are intense and personal, but the best of them evoke feelings and aspirations common to all men. The poem 'Freetown' works like this and so too does the poem 'Guinea'. Here, Cheney-Coker captures what we might call the spirit of revolutionary fervour:

> they had hoped to enslave the peasants of Guinea
> as they did four centuries ago
> but oh the invincible armies of Alpha Yaya

down the mountains of Foutah Djallon
and my heart lights up
like a burning flame in the night. . . . (p. 37)

Readers will find many such fine passages in these poems.

The poem 'Myopia' contains a section which exhibits Cheney-Coker's very distinctive use of imagery. It is the second section of the poem:

the boulevards of this country
are railway tracks in my heart
a train of anguish runs on them
rage corollary of hunger
the ricepads of this country
are putrid marshlands in my soul
tended by no magic fertilizers. . . . (p. 30)

The images, especially as they are used in this way, tend to objectify the poet's personal feelings. The 'train of anguish' image is very dramatic and forceful. Indeed, it could be said that this one image energises the whole poem. Another poem which greatly appeals to me is called 'Agony of the Dark Child'. Here we have a dramatic situation portrayed without ornament and without rhetoric. A child is born but, unfortunately, his relations realise that he is too 'dark'. They try to lighten his skin colour by using special chemicals and ointments. It is the irony behind the poem which gives it its peculiar power; the rejection of a child even by those nearest to him.

Trouble only comes for the poet when the image system breaks down, when the flood of thoughts and ideas refuses to order itself into a poem. (The problem is a little exacerbated, in this volume, by the reworking of certain basic images into various poems. We sometimes feel, I think, that they have been transferred too easily, without any creative modification.) The poem 'The Crucified' exemplifies these difficulties. There is, simply, too much in it, too many thoughts, ideas and images which refuse to be governed by the logic of the poem itself. The poem fairly bristles with these thoughts and images, but they operate so as to prevent the reader ever coming to terms with them, rather than drawing him in towards the central experience of the poem. The result is a certain confusion in the reader's mind, and also a sense of urgent creative energy 'untamed'.

Readers themselves might wish to search for analogues to these poems in the work of certain African, American, and South American poets. But, it would seem to me that this poetry is both distinctive and individual. Despite the criticism levelled in my last paragraph, the poetic felicities contained in *Concerto for an Exile* promise much for the future. It is to be hoped that Syl Cheney-Coker continues to speak, and to write, distinctively.

Yulisa Amadu Maddy
No Past, No Present, No Future

Eustace Palmer

Yulisa Amadu Maddy, *No Past, No Present, No Future*, African Writers
Series, Heinemann, 1973.

The most recent addition to the steadily growing corpus of Sierra Leonean
literature is Yulisa Amadu Maddy's *No Past, No Present, No Future*, the
story of three young Sierra Leoneans whose friendship is destroyed by
their personal weakness, by the exigencies of study in a foreign country,
and (so the author will have us believe) by the complicated social structure
of their native Sierra Leone (called Bauya in the novel). As the title
implies, *No Past, No Present, No Future* is a bleak study of rootlessness,
frustrated ambition, wasted opportunity, aimlessness and gloom. Its three
young heroes, having cut themselves off, for one reason or another, from
their roots in the past, still find themselves unable to cope with the demands
of the present, and the author holds out no hope for them in the future.

Joe Bengoh, Ade John and Santigie Bombolai are generally representative of the hordes of Sierra Leonean drop-outs who during the late
'50s and early '60s, made their way to the United Kingdom by fair means
or foul and scrambled, with the aid of menial jobs as porters, dish-washers
or whatever, to schools of drama or journalism, or careers as actors and
entertainers. Some managed to return with certificates of some sort.
Others, largely because of woefully inadequate qualifications, became
miserable failures.

The events of the novel start with Joe Bengoh joining the other two at
the Roman Catholic Mission in the capital after the horrifying death of
his parents. The friendship thus forged receives its first setback when,
shortly before the G.C.E. examinations, both Ade and Santigie are forced
to interrupt their education, the former because he has made a girl preg-
nant, the latter because of the untimely death of his father. Joe Bengoh
takes the examination successfully, but he later wrong-headedly gives up
his studies and joins the other two at their railway jobs. Together they
amass money, through the most corrupt practices, to sail for England.

Once in England, however, the friendship which has already been strained by tribal tensions, is unable to survive the rigours of study in an alien environment, and the three drift apart. Santigie becomes an academic failure and decides to take revenge by exploiting British women; Joe Bengoh becomes neurotically irresponsible and is expelled from his college. Ade succeeds academically, only to discover that he has ruined his chances of harmonious relationships through his lies and callousness.

The presentation of Freetown society is an essential part of Maddy's purpose, since he must demonstrate that the stifling, ultraconservative nature of the city is primarily responsible for the boys' thwarted ambition and ultimately for the breakdown of their friendship. Appropriately therefore, the first part of the novel, which is unquestionably the best, is a powerful evocation of Freetown, particularly of Creole society. Drawing richly from his own experience of life in the capital, Maddy has been able to recreate scenes which many Sierra Leoneans will recognise as familiar. Indeed this is likely to be one of the reasons for the book's appeal.

To say, however, that the book is a powerful and vivid evocation of Freetown life, is not to say that it is an accurate or faithful one, and it will be unfortunate if foreign readers are led to believe that it gives as faithful a picture of social or political realities in Sierra Leone as *The Beautyful Ones* has given of Ghana and *A Man of the People* of Nigeria. For the distortions, falsifications, and confusion of detail are all too glaring.

This is particularly evident in the author's treatment of the theme of tribalism. The reader forms the impression that Maddy is an extremely angry man – angry, that is, with what he feels are the basic assumptions and characteristics of Creole society, and he unfortunately allows his anger and prejudices to cloud his objectivity and to blind him to the need for critical and intellectual rigour in the analysis of so complex a problem. The agent he uses to voice his contempt for Creole society is Joe Bengoh, a neurotic, ultra-sensitive creature with mule-headed complexes, whose inability to penetrate and understand Creole society has left him with an enormous chip on his shoulder. Maddy's handling of a crucial incident is significant. Mary, a girl of provincial origins living with Creole guardians, has been punished in an old-fashioned Creole way for naughtiness. Joe Bengoh, displaying his neurotic touchiness sees this as one more instance of Creole tyranny towards provincial wards. Subsequently Joe and Ade meet Mary who, like them, has come upstream to do her laundry. Joe, who has had no prior sexual experience, is aroused and wonders whether this girl, who has been reputed to go to bed with every Tom, Dick and Harry, will oblige him. He makes advances and the girl succumbs; but Ade, who has been watching them, demands his turn with threats, and Mary succumbs again. The sensitive Joe immediately construes this as another example of Creole tyranny; he thinks he is seeing the real Creole Ade for the first time – an Ade who must secretly despise him and Santigie. But there is not the slightest evidence in the scene as presented to support the view that Ade's motives were tribalistic. If Ade has been beastly to Mary, so has Joe; both have merely exploited her for their own purposes, and there is nothing to suggest that the latter has a higher opinion of the girl than the former. Unfortunately, Joe allows the feelings derived from this event to throw a cloud over the whole relationship and ultimately to destroy it. But what is disastrous for the book as art is that there could be no mistaking in the uncritical presentation of Joe Bengoh, the fund of sympathy existing between him and his creator.

Maddy is equally uncritical in his presentation of the relations existing between the three youths and the society in which they find themselves. He no doubt sees Sierra Leone society as narrow-minded, meddlesome, and unimaginative, and he relates with great gusto and sympathy the various acts of rebellion of his three heroes as he conducts them on their rake's progress of drinking, whoring, promiscuity, and corruption. In so doing he comes very close to endorsing insubordination, filial ingratitude and moral degeneracy. Maddy blinds himself to his characters' responsibility for their catastrophe, attributing it instead to a hypocritical Sierra Leone and an equally hypocritical Britain. The fact is that Joe, Ade, and Santigie are a trio of tiresome irresponsibles behaving as though they belonged to the worst elements of Sierra Leone society. And yet Maddy's sympathy remains with them. It remains with Ade when in an act of revenge against his boss, the goods inspector, he steals a whole consignment of goods, in consequence of which the goods inspector is reduced to second-class station master and transferred to a remote area, while Ade goes off to England; it remains with the irresponsible Joe Bengoh as he wallows in the arms of prostitutes, steals a diamond and sells it for £6,000, squanders the money in loose living, samples all sorts of perversions in Paris and eventually becomes a hippie-type drug addict and homosexual in England; and it remains with Santigie who, having failed academically, debases himself by virtually becoming a male prostitute. Such is the quality of the author's moral evaluation.

Maddy's handling of language is at best amateurish. Even after making allowances for the African writer's problems in writing in English, a language not of his own choosing and which is often inadequate to accommodate his insights, one is still struck by the linguistic incompetence of *No Past, No Present, No Future*. Maddy's attempts at reproducing Krio speech on paper are often quite ludicrous, and this is not just due to the difficulty of establishing an orthographic convention for Krio. Most Krio speakers will easily recognise his version of their language as pidgin rather than Krio. Maddy is no more fortunate in his handling of standard English, as the inelegance of this sentence demonstrates: 'Quietly they walked under the dim lights that threw a half light in the dark and dangerous night, haunted by ghosts, in which thieves and tramps and dogs paraded'. Who is haunted by ghosts, and what do the thieves and tramps and dogs parade in? Or this one: 'She knew they were mostly drunk to know what they were doing.'

Yet, in spite of its flaws, which also include historical and sociological confusion and spurious psychology, *No Past, No Present, No Future*, does not deserve to be merely dismissed as a rather ineptly written apologia for decadence and irresponsibility. There are some superbly realised scenes such as those in the brothel and the railway freight office. The characterisation, particularly that of Joe Bengoh, is often quite subtle and convincing. All things considered, it is a useful addition to the corpus of Sierra Leonean literature.

Index

168

9 781847 011206

Lightning Source UK Ltd.
Milton Keynes UK
UKHW02f1153131117
312665UK00007B/739/P

9 781847 011206